I Pray t/
a blessing
bountiful for
living.

Sandra Burnett
I BELIEVE GOD!

Bountiful Blessings in Believing

Victorious Living Begins with Believing

SANDRA BURNETT

Wasteland Press
www.wastelandpress.net
Shelbyville, KY USA

Bountiful Blessings in Believing:
Victorious Living Begins with Believing
by Sandra Burnett

Copyright © 2020 Sandra Burnett
ALL RIGHTS RESERVED

First Printing – September 2020
ISBN: 978-1-68111-360-9

NO PART OF THIS BOOK MAY BE REPRODUCED IN
ANY FORM, BY PHOTOCOPYING OR BY ANY ELECTRONIC
OR MECHANICAL MEANS, INCLUDING INFORMATION
STORAGE OR RETRIEVAL SYSTEMS, WITHOUT PERMISSION
IN WRITING FROM THE COPYRIGHT OWNER/AUTHOR

Printed in the U.S.A.

0   1   2   3   4

This Book is dedicated to all those who want to know God and understand that something which gnaws at your mind and heart, and you are just not sure what that pull is. You're missing something in your life. You struggle to put your finger on just what that missing piece could be. Some of you are very satisfied in the natural with finances, possessions, family, and even with strong, fulfilling relationships. Still, you feel empty. There is something else that you need.

Others are still making their way, striving to achieve the house, wealth, family, and security. Beyond the natural necessities and our desires, there's an undercurrent of unsatisfied want and need, which tugs at you. What is it? All of us, at some stage in our life, will find that our soul longs for God. You don't believe that, or you're not sure? There is a scripture in the Bible that says, **"My soul thirsteth for God, for the living God: when shall I come and appear before God?" Psalm 42:2.**

Take this literary journey with me and discover what your soul needs to quench its thirst. We will discuss many things, including the existence of God, our ability to trust God, and His Holy Spirit. I encourage you to open your mind and heart as you embark upon this journey with me. You are sure to be blessed!

ACKNOWLEDGEMENT

I give praise and honor to my Heavenly Father, whom my soul thirsts after just as a deer for flowing streams. Thank you for saving me at the tender age of thirteen. Your love is priceless, unfailing, and your intimate presence is my comfort and resting place.

This book is in loving memory of my classy mother (Mama) Frances Jean Juniel, who transitioned from this life to glory on September 12th, 2015. I love you Mama. I miss you so much, and I'll always cherish the precious memories I have of you. I'm grateful to you for pushing me to do better and showing me how to be a strong independent woman through your hard work ethics, diligence, and determination.

This book is dedicated to my uncle, Lloyd Rideout, who God used as the catalyst to bring me to the saving knowledge of Jesus Christ at a very young age.

I dedicate this book to my husband, who has been my best friend, shown me unconditional love, been my inspiration, and my number one supporter in ministry. Through every challenge, he's continued to support my efforts as I move forward in the things of God. Thank you for being a loving husband and a great father to our handsome sons Joshua, Jonathan, and Jordon. Thank you for teaching them the love of God, the way to God, and the fear of God. Love You Forever! I also thank God for my two granddaughters, Aaliyah and Faith. Words cannot express how much I love you, and how proud I am to be called your grandmother.

FOREWORD

I had the honor of meeting Sandra Burnett (Sandy) when I was just 12 years old. She was 13 at that time. I had never seen anyone as mature in their walk with Christ. I was a new believer, but I couldn't help but notice Sandra's love for God. At such a young age, her commitment to Christ was unmatched by her peers, and her desire to grow in His word was undeniable. Sandra was a special young lady and those of us fortunate enough to be in her circle wanted to love God as she did. Sandra never took the small things for granted. Every opportunity was seen as a blessing from God no matter how great or small, she always gave God the glory, and today she still does.

We live in a culture where many struggle to keep their faith in God alive. Gone are the days when people believed just because mama or grandma told them to. It doesn't matter that they have spent the majority of their lives in a church; somehow, things just don't seem to make sense anymore. The core of our belief system is challenged by today's culture. The world is in search of what's really real. They want and need to know that what they believe is right.

It's not strange that over 40 years after meeting Sandra, she would be writing a book on the subject of believing God. This is her life's testimony. Down through the years, Sandra has modeled someone who stood in the face of adversity, knowing and trusting God with her life. Her prayer life, as well as her love life, has set her apart as a woman filled with the wisdom and knowledge of God. The book you are reading is proof of this fact, Sandra can be trusted. Her life matches her conversation, and I'm honored to know Sandra and together we pray that the fullness of God's plan will be in operation in her life.

Melva L. Henderson
Founder/Vice President
World Outreach & Bible Training Center

INTRODUCTION OF AUTHOR

From DREAM…
　　Everything starts with an idea or concept in your mind.
　　　　To DRAWING…
　　　　　　The dream is given form by putting it on paper.
　　　　　　To REALITY…
　　　　　　　　The construction process begins.

From now to the end of time, people will continue to discuss and debate the existence and power of God. Because of my passion for God and desire to continue to grow and nurture my relationship with Him, I am not easily satisfied by superficial material. Dr. Sandra Burnett did not disappoint me. Her in-depth, clear, and personal walk down avenues of faith-based topics that confuse most were very enriching, informative, and engaging. I wanted to read more and more. I felt as if I was being spoon-fed delicious bites of God's heart, His nature, and His character, which made me feel close to the Lord. The book stirred my interest, pulled me in, and made me want to read further to know what was next. I learned, laughed, and prayed as I enjoyed the engaging spiritual awakening.

I want to congratulate Dr. Sandra Burnett on one of her many books, which she will publish. I believe her books will be a tremendous blessing to the body of Christ. It is truly an honor, and privilege, to write this foreword. I have been blessed to be married to her for over thirty years. She is the first lady of my life, and the mother of my three sons, Joshua, Jonathan and Jordan.

She is truly an anointed woman of God with a challenging, exhorting, and encouraging message to the church. Dr. Burnett is a dynamic preacher and teacher of the *Word* of God. Her book ***Bountiful Blessings In Believing*** is not only a relevant and insightful book, but it is also vital for 21st-century believers.

If you desire to make a bigger and better impact on the kingdom of God, I highly recommend this book, which will embrace and drive the reader to a deeper and more vibrant faith. She shares her life experiences and testimonials of how she was able to overcome challenges, keep the faith, and believe God through the greatest of circumstances. It will equip the reader with tips and tools on how to live victoriously and believe God when your faith is under attack.

While the great Apostle Paul was in the midst of one of the greatest storms of his life, the Euroclydon, he declared to the men on the ship, "Wherefore, sirs, be of good cheer: for I believe God, that it shall be even as it was told to me," Acts 27:25. Get ready for an exciting journey as you read ***Bountiful Blessings In Believing***. You will be encouraged to declare even as the great Apostle Paul did powerful, bold, courageous, and anointed proclamations from the Word of God that will pave a path to your deliverance and rich blessings amid life's storms.

Much love,
Husband
Pastor Lawrence Burnett
Grace Christian Fellowship Church,
Milwaukee, WI

CONTENTS

FOREWORD vii

INTRODUCTION OF AUTHOR ix

CHAPTER ONE: *Do You Believe God?* 1

CHAPTER TWO: *God Is A Spirit* 13

CHAPTER THREE: *Only Believe* 21

CHAPTER FOUR: *I Believe Even When He Is Quiet* 33

CHAPTER FIVE: *I Believe God And The Power Of Prayer* 42

CHAPTER SIX-A: *Train Your Human Spirit To Believe God* 49

CHAPTER SIX-B: *Train Your Human Spirit To Believe God* 64

CHAPTER SEVEN: *Take Heed Of Your Associates* 77

CHAPTER EIGHT: *Believe God For Bigger Better* 88

CHAPTER ONE
Do You Believe God?

Many too many people have asked the same question over thousands of years. "Do you believe in God?" People ponder many things along that path of thought. God is not a physical being that you can see, hear, or touch is a common debate used to deny the existence of God. People find it difficult to believe in things that they cannot explain, things that defy human understanding. Things that cross over into the realm of the supernatural are typically very difficult for people to wrap their minds around. You must be willing to consider at least that there is a powerful source beyond what we can see that created this world and governs it supernaturally.

People often find it easier to believe the "Big Bang" theory as an explanation of how the world came into existence. The theory suggests that some 10 to 20 billion years ago, a massive blast allowed all the universe's known matter and energy—even space and time themselves—to spring from some ancient and unknown type of energy. That theory makes it easier for people to dispel the concept of an Almighty God.

Believing in the supernatural and looking past the limits that are in the natural require more effort, more thought, and the ability to challenge what is easy and go deeper.

I get excited when people ask me, "How do you know that God exists?" It excites me because in my mind the proof of God's existence embraces us with a gentle touch of amazement every day. The bright sun which illuminates the sky and is a necessity for plant life to exist tells me that there is a God. The moon and the stars that command the night, and know the place they are to appear in the sky without fail, in a galaxy that no physical man can control, tells me that there is a God. The rivers that flow into the depths of the sea and travel in one direction needing no help from humankind, speak to the existence of God. The glorious seas and oceans that host a completely different world filled with life that lives in the deep speak to an awesome power. Let's not forget the wind's whisper that whistles through the tree leaves, blades of grass, even the flowers, and commands them to bow down and worship the creator. All these magnificent wonders of the world defy the concept of the "Big Bang" theory.

No burst of energy, which is incapable of having a mind or any level of intelligence, could have sculpted the beautiful intricate world in which we live. The *Word* of God tells us, *"For by him all things were created, that are in heaven, and that are in earth, visible and invisible, whether they be thrones, or dominions, or principalities, or powers: all things were created by him and for him," Colossians 1:16.*

Nature, the earth, mountains, volcanoes, waterfalls, and all the natural phenomenon, which humans did not create, offer proof that there is a God. There is a supernatural force in this world that supersedes the ability of humans. The intelligence of mankind is but a feeble thought that has no strength compared to the omniscient God. The Word of God makes that very proclamation. *"For my thoughts are not your thoughts, neither are your ways my ways, saith the LORD. For as the heavens are higher than the earth, so are my ways higher than your ways, and my thoughts than your thoughts;"* Read it for yourself in *Isaiah 55: 8-9*.

Just like you believe man went to the moon and that there is a planet called Jupiter in the galaxy, you have to choose to believe that there is a God. Everything in this world, you will not be able to touch with your hands or see it with your eyes. But you believe it, and you trust that it exists. The belief in God is no different. You must open your mind and heart, then look around you and take in the beauty of all that God has created for our pleasure. And surely consider the miraculous things that have happened in your life that you or no one else can explain. Maybe you or someone you love survived an accident that should have been sure death. Perhaps you or someone you love is a cancer survivor. Just take a few minutes, close your eyes, and in your mind, walk back over the course of your life. I am confident that you will find something that happened to you that was out of your control and out of the control of any human being. That thing you can't explain, that good thing, it was a blessing, and it was because of God.

As I sat before the Father, I sought His wisdom concerning His people. I wanted to know why so many in the Body of Christ fall short of realizing the promises of His *Word*. The Holy Spirit revealed to me that people lack the faith needed to simply believe God. Unfortunately, this self-imposed inability to simply take God at His *Word* is commonplace in the Church today. Instead of simply believing God, many have more confidence in their flesh and in the power of Satan.

They lack the faith to trust God and tap into the spiritual things of God. Their belief is only in what they can see and experience in the natural.

The born again believer cannot embrace that weak mindset because in God, the Spirit is dominant and more powerful than the natural. The Father declares Himself responsible for fulfilling His Word. He holds you responsible to only believe. Your walk of faith demands that you avoid taking counsel from your flesh but believe God and take Him at His *Word*.

Point of Grace: It is not your mind that believes God; it is your Spirit man. The mind must be renewed according to *Ephesians 4:23, "And be renewed in the spirit of your mind."* The Bible gives a very clear description of faith: *"Now faith is the substance of things hoped for, the evidence of things not seen," Hebrews 11:1.*

Faith doesn't make sense to our narrow natural way of thinking. In the natural, we trust what we can see and even then sometimes still require a scientific explanation. We must step out of the natural and into the supernatural in order to take a stand to believe in God and trust God. There is no correlation between what we can see, hear, touch, taste or smell as it relates to God. Those sensory things are relevant in the natural world. However, those senses that we depend on in the natural are irrelevant in the Spiritual realm.
But we are able to experience the goodness and blessings of God and feel His presence, because of His Holy Spirit. I love this Bible verse, *"O taste and see that the Lord is good: blessed is the man that trusteth in him," Psalm 34:8.*

Our flesh operates strictly within the realm of human reasoning. Meaning, things that are logical, explainable by science, or if we can see it, the mind finds it easy to believe or accept. But faith requires you to believe that which is not always explainable. You cannot see it, and there is no scientific explanation for it, which can appease the human mind. Those who have faith can operate in the Spirit realm and trust in God for that which they have not seen and man struggles to understand.

Consider This:

Jesus told Jairus, the ruler of the synagogue, *"Only believe," Luke 8:50.* His daughter was dead. Jesus had the power to raise the child from the dead as if she had only been asleep. Jesus challenged Jairus to believe that the child who was dead could live again. So this grieving father had to look and believe beyond what was before him in the natural. And beyond what he understood. Death was not a stranger, uncommon, or unbelievable. The concept of Jairus' daughter being brought back to life was not as easy to understand or believe. The father, who had just been told that his daughter was dead, had to believe in Jesus and His power, which was beyond the natural abilities of a man. We will examine this great teaching moment in more depth in a later chapter.

"Be not afraid, only believe." Jesus emphasized that Jairus needed to have faith. Walking by faith means that you reinforce your thinking with actions that showcase your trust in the authority and power of God's *Word*. We must live our lives by that authority even when what we are trusting God for has not yet come to pass in our lives. It means refusing to fear anything that conflicts with the authority of God's *Word*.

In order to walk by faith, you must live each day, setting your mind on things above rather than on worldly reasoning. Whatever you believe God for, a house, a job, a spouse, no matter what it is, don't waiver. Stand firm, unmoved by the perceptions of your senses.

Remember, God hastens over His *Word* to perform it. He is not a man that He should lie to us, and His ways are not our ways. You can trust God.

How Do I Establish My Belief and Trust in God? Glad You Asked:

We establish our belief in God and build our trust in Him by pouring ourselves over His *Word*. The Bible is an oasis of **Truth**, **Power**, **Knowledge**, and a **Source** to empower you to intimately know the heart of God. We read and trust textbooks, newspapers, magazines, television, and even the internet to inform and educate us. God's *Word* is the only legitimate source that leads us to the true and living God. It is trustworthy because God Himself inspired righteous men to pen His Holy *Word*. *"All scripture is given by inspiration of God, and it is profitable for doctrine, for reproof, for correction, for instruction in righteousness…"* *2nd Timothy 3:16.*

The Bible was written by (Holy inspiration) given to over 30 men and took thousands of years to write. What other books on the face of the earth have a profound thread of continuity woven throughout from page to page, by multiple
authors, without a single word of contradiction? Not one! No, not one! Look at the power of God. Only God could have orchestrated such a rich book anointed with truth and power, and it all rest within the same garment of sacred scriptures, called the Bible.

Your faith in God has to be built on something. That foundation has to be the *Word* of God. So you must hear it and read it. When I say to hear it, I mean you need to hear the *Word* of God preached, taught, and explained to you that it might prick your heart, and you will begin to thirst for more and more knowledge about God. *"So then faith cometh by hearing, and hearing by the word of God," Romans 10:17.* This scripture confirms for us that we need God's *Word* in order to have faith in Him. God's *Word*, His Bible, is so powerful that it can change your life, your way of thinking, and show you yourself in a way only God can.

The content of God's *Word* awakens faith in us. That is how powerful the *Word* of God is. That is the intent of His *Word*. It will show you the loving God that He is and open your heart and mind to the many blessings that He has for you. When you hear the *Word*, and it begins to take root in your heart and mind, that is when your faith in God begins to grow, and a change in you starts to take place.

Now, hearing is not enough. You need to read for yourself and confirm that what you are hearing or being taught is correct, according to the *Word* of God, not your own beliefs. God wants us to pour ourselves over His *Word*, which He left for us that our hearts and souls might be fed. The scripture tells us, *"Man shall not live by bread alone, but by every word that proceedeth out of the mouth of God," Matthew 4:4. We can hear it with our natural ear, but we must also hear it with our heart,* which means to trust the *Word*, confess it out of your mouth, and it will take hold in your mind, and you will believe. Faith in God and His *Word* will be the end result.

Keep in mind that the power in the hearing of God's *Word* is not just the words themselves. The *Word* of God has power because it is entrenched in the Holy Spirit. And it is God's Spirit that speaks to the heart of man that brings about faith and a changed life. **What is the Holy Spirit?** Don't worry; we will talk about that in another chapter. I'm excited about the discussion.

Your faith is established and grows by reading the *Word* of God and living your life according to it. As your faith grows and God's Holy Spirit impacts you, your heart, mind, and your will begins to conform to the very *Word* of God. You will find peace and pleasure in reading the *Word* of God and allowing it to blossom in your life. It will change what and how you believe and mold your actions into obedience to God's *Word*.

Your mind and life will take on a pleasing new outlook. For example:

1. If you believe God created the institution of marriage, you won't commit adultery, **Hebrews 13:4.**
2. If you believe sexual sin is a work of the flesh, you won't fornicate, **Galatians 5:19.**
3. If you believe by the stripes of Christ you are healed, you'll confess your healing, 1st **Peter 2:24.**
4. If you believe God has not given you a Spirit of fear, you'll operate out of power and a sound mind, 2nd **Timothy 1:7.**
5. If you believe stealing from God leaves you cursed with a curse, you'll happily release the tithes, **Malachi 3:8-10.**
6. If you believe God is a Spirit, you will worship Him in Spirit and in truth, **St. John 4:24.**
7. Do you believe God hates lying lips? If you desire to please God, you will not lie, **Proverbs 12:22.**
8. Do you believe you shall receive anything you ask the Father for in Jesus' name? Then pray in the name of Jesus, **St. John 14:13-14.**

See, it's that simple. When you believe, your actions reflect your convictions. Whatever you think, speak, and do are manifestations of what you believe. When you believe God, your thoughts, words, and actions will line up with the truth. That is how you experience the promises of God manifested in your life, along with righteous living, of course. And that is made possible by the Holy Spirit.

Now that we understand how our faith is established, takes root in our heart, then grows and matures into the very actions that drive our lives, let's consider some of the fruits of having faith in God.

I love to talk about how good God is and how the **Good Hand** of God operates in my life. Let me share a couple of testimonies with you:

My husband and I decided to believe God for a brand new home, which we would build from the ground up. We trusted Him that it would have a fireplace and that each of our three sons would have their own bedroom. So I started speaking in faith what I wanted to see manifest in the natural. During that time, we were living in a tiny three-bedroom home, and our three sons were sleeping in the same room. Even with both of our annual income combined, it seemed impossible that we could build a home. But with God, all things are possible. We needed a supernatural blessing.

Believing God is a Kingdom of God Principle. Belief in the promises of God is the key that unlocks and moves the promises of God into the natural realm. That requires believing God, no matter what. For years, we consistently spoke with faith in God just what we wanted to see manifest in the natural, our brand new five-bedroom home.

So vividly, I remember our oldest son, who was seven or eight years old at the time, asking me, "Mama, when are we going to build our home?" To me, he was really saying, "I heard you say many times, we are going to build a house, but when?" I answered him with confidence, "I don't know when, but we are going to do it."

I held onto my faith in God and His promises to bless me if I was willing and obedient, *Isaiah 1:19*. I refused to allow my circumstances and what I could only see in the natural to hinder my faith. God rewarded steadfast diligence in my trusting Him. My husband was driving and saw a subdivision of new homes being built. He decided to stop at one of the model homes and inquire about having a house built. The person he spoke with did some calculations and based on our small income said, "You and your wife can build a house." Look at God! Less than two years later, and we had just what we'd believed God for. We built our own home from the ground up with a fireplace, and each of our sons had their own bedroom. Trust God and stand on His *Word*. Just like He worked a miracle for us, He can work one for you.

Allow me to share one more brief testimony to the goodness of the Lord. When we step out in faith and believe God, we will experience the impossible. My husband and I were interested in a small building. The owner of the property asked us to make him an offer. We knew nothing about this man and had just met him for the first time that day. Suddenly, I heard the Lord say to me, "Tell him to give you the building for free." That sounded crazy to me. Let me tell you, believing God for the supernatural will cause you to say and do things that don't make sense to you.

Trusting God in this instance took a big leap of faith for me because I was still learning the voice of God. I was still learning how to believe God for the supernatural. God's *Word* says, *"Ask, and you shall receive...," John 16:24*. My husband and I stepped away to discuss what to offer the man. I told him what God had told me. My husband went to the owner and said, "Give us the building for free." To the one and only true God, let there be glory. This man, who was a total stranger, called us back and said, "I want to give you the building for free." He did just that and signed the building over to us.

That is the kind of God that I serve. He is able to do exceeding abundantly above all that we ask, *Ephesians 3:20*. No way would we have considered asking the owner to give us his building for free. But God had a supernatural blessing for us. We just had to trust God enough to speak the words, which He had spoken to me. It seemed crazy to even think about telling this man to give us the building for free. There is nothing and no one in this universe that has the power of God. I tell you with all certainty, and not one ounce of doubt, there is a God. And when you accept that and get to know Him, you will shout it from the rooftop, "God is good, and He is real!"

"Lord, You are the water that quenches my thirst. It is You, Lord, who satisfies the needs of my flesh and my Spirit." That is how I feel about the Lord. That is what I tell the Lord when I pray. Once you believe in the Almighty God, and you start to commune with God in prayer, your inner man, which is your spirit, will be compelled to touch and communicate with God. The Holy Spirit is our one to one connection to God.

As we continue our journey through the pages of this book, which I pray will bless you, please keep in mind that it takes faith and trust to believe in God and grow in Him. Please consider the below two Bible verses that I hope you will find encouraging.

"O God, thou art my God; early will I seek thee: my soul thirsteth for thee, my flesh longeth for thee in a dry and thirsty land, where no water is," Psalm 63:1.

"Ye are my witnesses, saith the LORD, and my servant whom I have chosen: that ye may know and believe me, and understand that I am he: before me there was no God formed, neither shall there be after me," Isaiah 43:10.

<u>Prayer</u> - Precious and Righteous God – Lord bless those that ride the waves of uncertainty regarding Your existence and their inability to trust You. Bless them Lord out of the richness of Your Love, Grace,
and Power to have the opportunity
to experience You and to love You.
Lord, heal their unbelief.
In Jesus Name, Amen!

CHAPTER TWO
God Is A Spirit

Thank you for taking the journey into chapter 2 with me. In chapter 1, we established that it is essential for us to **Believe God,** and our faith in Him must grow. In our effort to know God, build our faith in Him, **Believe God**, and have closeness with Him, it is important for us to believe and understand that **God is a Spirit.** And we connect with Him through our spirit. The Bible tells us, *"God is a Spirit: and they that worship him must worship him in spirit and in truth," St. John 4:24.* Without the spiritual nature that God created in us, it would be impossible to worship him in the spirit. God is a Spirit, and when He made us in His own likeness, He also gave us a spirit.

What do you think? Let's talk about it.

Man is made in the image of God and after His likeness. We know the oneness of God is manifested in three parts, which we need to be clear on, (Father, Son, and Holy Spirit), but they are one God. Likewise, man is made up of three parts, <u>Spirit, Soul and Body</u>.

The *Word* of God clearly makes that distinction when Apostle Paul wrote, *"Now may the God of peace Himself sanctify you entirely; and may your spirit and soul and body be preserved complete, without blame at the coming of our Lord Jesus Christ," 1st Thessalonians 5:23.*

Let's go a little deeper into the makeup of man who God created.

<u>**The Spirit of Man**</u> - I like how Kenneth Copeland explains the Spirit. He said, "God communicates to our spirit and our spirit communicates what we hear to our mind (soul, will, intellect, desires), which is our soul." That to me is pretty clear. God communicates or talks to man through our spirit, which then transfers that communication to our mind. Understanding that man has a spirit helps us to understand that God communicates and fellowships with man through man's spirit. The Apostle Paul refers to our spirit also as the inward man, the inner person and the heart of man. We read in ***Proverbs 20:27***, *"The spirit of man is the candle of the Lord, searching all the inward parts of the belly."*

You see, when God breathed into the nostrils of man and gave him life, ***Genesis 2:7***, He also gave him a spirit. Again, making us in His own image. Our spirit is like a candle given to us by God as an inward light and guide to direct us along a path that He has designed for each of us. That inward light, (our spirit) allows God to search us deeply and know our thoughts, feelings, and yes, even our desires. The reference above to searching the inward parts of the belly is referring to the heart of man.

Our spirit wants to obey God since it was given to us by God. The spirit of man is our direct and binding connection to God. Therefore, it wants to be obedient to God. However, we must desire and allow our spirit man to be nurtured and grow strong in order for our spirit to direct our flesh to be obedient to God.

The spirit is that still voice which bubbles up from within the core of you. It seeps into your mind, and then it is a conscious thought that you can't shake. The Spirit of God speaks to your spirit, and the thoughts in your mind become your actions. It is then that you have made a choice to be led by God.

Romans 8:14 says, "For as many as are led by the Spirit of God, they are the sons of God." For me, this verse makes the connection between the Spirit of God and the spirit of man. When we choose to be led by the Spirit of God, we are acknowledging and accepting that innate connection to God, which He blessed man with, a spirit. Yet, it is our choice to latch on, give over, and hold onto that connection that God instilled in us, since God gave us free will.

<u>Point of Grace:</u> It is our spirit that provides us with that powerful binding, which ties us to God. When we are connected to God, washed in His blood, and endowed with His Holy Spirit, we have life and purpose beyond the grave, because we look forward to eternal life with God. When we choose to be led by God, we can then be called the Sons of God.

It takes more than the natural man (our mind and intelligence) to understand the things of God and the heart and mind of God. It requires a spiritual connection to God.

Yes, God made us in His image, and the spirit that He placed in us must be ignited by the Holy Spirit of God.

It is the Spirit of God that gives us an understanding of the things of God. And it drives our internal pull to God. Sometimes we may not know what the thing inside of us is that cultivates an empty feeling that nothing you do or achieve seems to satisfy. That gnawing, indescribable ache, and sense of incompletion is your spirit's desire to be intimate with God. Sometimes we listen to that feeling, and we allow it to lead us to God and rest there. Sometimes we don't listen; we continue to struggle against that Spiritual pull, and we walk outside of the purpose and path that God is calling us to.

In the famous words of Saint Augustine, the early Christian theologian, "Thou hast created us for Thyself, O God, and our hearts are restless until they find their rest in Thee!" We need the Spirit of God, His Holy Spirit, to work in us and regenerate our spirit. We need it to renew our mind and empower us to walk in the newness of life and become a new creature in Christ. It is then that we will have the desire to be like Christ and live according to His *Word*. When we do that, we are emulating God, who created us in His own Spiritual image.

<u>The Soul of Man</u> - *Genesis 2:7 states, "And the Lord God formed man of the dust of the ground, and breathed into his nostrils the breath of life; and man became a living soul."* Each of us are known as human beings. We can relate to that and believe that. Believe also that human beings are souls. The soul of man hosts the mind and our conscience. It is the root or essence of what makes you internally different than the next person. It is our soul that enables us to feel guilty about something that we may regret having done or said. It is the barometer of our actions, which defines for us if something is right or wrong.

God made it clear in His *Word* that the soul is His and that the soul will bear consequences. *"Behold, all souls are mine; as the soul of the father, so also the soul of the son is mine: the soul that sinneth, it shall die," Ezekiel 18:4.* God's *Word* is so rich and filled with knowledge and understanding meant to help us.

<u>The Body of Man</u> - The body is the material part of man and where the five senses operate: sight, smell, hearing, taste, and touch. The body is the natural skin and bone that makes up the frame of flesh that we walk around in. Some of us are tall, while others are short. Some of us are shaped with a thin frame as others strut around with a fuller frame. Either way, God created us from the dust of the very earth that he commanded to take shape just by the sound of His voice. Isn't that remarkable? The elements and atmosphere obeyed His words. *Genesis 1:2, "And the earth was without form, and void; and the darkness was upon the face of the deep. And the Spirit of God moved upon the face of the waters." Genesis 1:9-10, "And God said, Let the waters under the heaven be gathered together unto one place, and let the dry land appear: and it was so. And God called the dry land earth..."*

God created us as three parts that together make the whole of who we are. The Spirit, Soul, and Body are all three important, but it is through our spirit that we can connect to God. And it is through our spirit that God dwells within us and connects with us. We can feel God, sense Him, and allow His Spirit to dwell within us.

When I think about the magnificent creation of man and the awesome world in which we live, I wonder about the mind and desire of God. Do you sometimes wonder why God created man? I think many people ask that question. Let's consider that mystery.

"When I consider your heavens, the work of your fingers, the moon and the stars, which thou has ordained; what is man that you are mindful of him, the son of man that you care for him?" Psalm 8:3-4.

"Then God said, Let us make mankind in our image, in our likeness, so that they may rule over the fish in the sea and the birds in the sky, over the livestock and all the wild animals, and all the creatures that move along the ground," Genesis 1:26.

God created us for this purpose. But He also created us to love Him and serve Him. God created you and me in His own image. It was His purpose that we know Him and feel the connection in our spirit that ties us to Him. To grow in the likeness of Him as we live and experience life and the love that He has for us. God desires that we reign with Him in eternal life because of the spirit that He gave each of us. We have the choice to follow the path that He designed for our lives. The path that directs us to allow God to use us to draw others unto Him; to love Him, and to show others the same Godly love that He shows each of us.

God is Holy, Perfect, and Righteous. He is a loving God. He made us in His image, which means innately we are fashioned in the image of those attributes. That is why as humans, we are drawn to the desire and need to be loved. We can love people who hurt us, love them that don't love us, and feel empty and lonely when we don't have the fulfillment of a companion to share our lives with. The love that God has for us compels us to desire love as well.

Because of the spirit that God gave man that draws us to Him, we feel lost, without peace, unfulfilled, and yes, sometimes empty when we do not answer the call of God. When He whispers to our soul, touches our spirit, and calls us unto Him, He is showing us that He loves us.

As we learn about God, accept that He is a Spirit, and began to understand that we must believe God beyond what we see, hear, and feel, we are ready to learn just how we build our trust and belief in God.

I love the *Word* of God. It is so fulfilling when you are hungry to know the heart of God. I spend time reading God's *Word* and pouring myself over it in order to have an intimate relationship with God and to know what He desires of me. His *Word* connects me to the heart of God. Yes, God is a Spirit, but we are able to connect to Him emotionally and spiritually. Because of that, we can know Him and have a personal relationship with Him. That personal relationship can be intimate and fulfilling. The Spirit of God makes that possible.

God wants us to worship Him in spirit and in truth and with our soul and our heart. God is worthy of our worship, and we should desire to feel His presence and His Spirit. I hope that you take away from this chapter a desire to reside in the presence of God and to have an intimate spiritual relationship with Him. *"God is a Spirit: and they that worship him must worship him in spirit and in truth," John 4:24.*

Below are just a few encouraging quotes from various prominent people that I would like for you to consider. Not all professed to be a Christian, but they all had very passionate views about God.

> "You were made by God and for God, and until you understand that, life will never make sense." **(Rick Warren)**

> "As believers in Jesus Christ, our work is to believe while God works on our behalf." **(Joyce Meyer)**

> "Take the first step in faith. You don't have to see the whole staircase, just take the first step."
>
> **(Martin Luther King, Jr.)**

"We may ignore, but we can nowhere evade the presence of God. The world is crowded with Him. He walks everywhere incognito." **(C.S. Lewis)**

"But for my faith in God,
I should have been a raving maniac."
(Mahatma Gandhi)

"Draw nigh to God, and He will draw nigh to you,"
James 4:8.

<u>Prayer</u> - Mighty and Gracious God, I give You praise and thank You for every blessing. You are a loving, kind, and forgiving God. Thank You for allowing me another day of life, and another opportunity to know You better, and to draw nigh unto thee. In Jesus Name, Amen!

CHAPTER THREE
Only Believe

The thread of continuity that you will see woven through each chapter of this book is the proclamation to **Believe God** beyond what you see, what you hear, and what you feel. The circumstances and the mountain of challenges that dare to stand before you should not shake your faith in God and what His *Word* assures you of. You must say to yourself, to that mountain of challenges, to that seemingly impossible situation, **I Believe God**.

You might be thinking that to say **I Believe God** and actually being able to put that proclamation into action are two different things. And you are right. Believing God does take a step of faith. But God is a great teacher, who shows us just how to believe in Him.

There are probably things that have taken place in your life where God was showing you why or how to believe in Him.

Jesus was often referred to as "Teacher" by His disciples and the multitudes that followed Him. Actually, over fifty times in the Gospels,

Jesus was referred to as "Teacher." More profound than that, Jesus called himself a teacher, *"You call me Teacher and Lord, and rightly so, for that is what I am," John 13:13.*

There are times in our lives when God allows good and bad things to happen in order to teach us that He and He alone is all powerful. He is showing us and teaching us that He is our source for all things, great and small. Those teaching opportunities are to show us His love for us, how powerful He is, and that He is capable of healing any situation in our lives. Jesus showed himself all-powerful, even beyond the clutches of death to the synagogue ruler, Jairus.

"O death, where is thy <u>sting</u>? O grave, where is thy <u>victory</u>?" This powerful scripture is found in *1ˢᵗ Corinthians 15:55.*

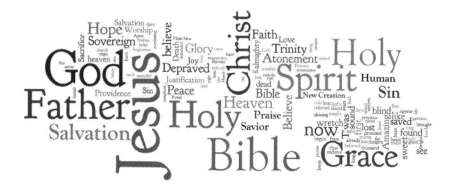

Let's consider the lesson that Jesus, **<u>The Great Teacher</u>**, taught Jairus. We talked a little bit about Jairus in chapter 1. We will dissect the account more here and pick apart the teaching moments that God used to show forth Jairus' faith while still taking him through a learning process to take his faith to another level. The account of Jairus and his ability to believe God is so encouraging. We find as we read in *Mark 5:22-23, "And, behold, there cometh one of the rulers of the synagogue,*

Jairus by name; and when he saw him, he fell at his feet, And besought him greatly, saying, My little daughter lieth at the point of death: I pray thee, come and lay thy hands on her, that she may be healed; and she shall live. And Jesus went with him; and much people followed him, and thronged him."

So the Jewish leader of the synagogue had heard of Jesus and His miraculous healing power. He went to Jesus and fell at His feet, believing that He had the power to heal is daughter, who was dying. Now this man hadn't met Jesus; he'd only heard of Him. Still, he believed in the power of Jesus and the marvelous wonders that He had done. Talk about Jesus and the miracles of healing and unexplainable wonders that amazed people were being heard all around the area.

This Biblical account makes me think about the fact that sometimes we find it hard to believe God for something even when He has already done such great things for us. He and He alone have delivered us from situations that only God could have possibly done. Yet there are still times when belief for us is difficult to muster up. Jairus, on the other hand, learned to believe Jesus for a hard thing.

As Jesus and Jairus walked along, the crowd followed them. Among the crowd was a woman who'd suffered from a bleeding disorder for twelve years. She had seen many physicians and spent all the money she had. The woman was now poor and still plagued with the bleeding disorder. There are many people who have suffered some type of major medical crisis while having sought after top specialist and spent a fortune only to continue to suffer with the same sickness. Many of us have struggled with a medical crisis that has altered our very lives. So we can understand how desperately the woman wanted to be healed.

The woman believed Jesus and all that she had heard about Him. Her belief; her faith in Jesus was so strong that she said,

"If I may touch but his clothes, I shall be whole," Mark 5:28. Isn't that type of faith amazing? It is that type of faith that many of us wish we had. Jesus responded immediately to her awesome display of faith. The Bible proclaims, *"And Straightway the fountain of her blood was dried up; and she felt in her body that she was healed of that plague," Mark 5:29.* The woman wasn't even trying to touch Jesus or have Him pray for her. She was content in just touching the hem of His garment and **believed** that she would be made whole.

Let's not forget that Jairus was walking along with Jesus. He was in the middle of the **Process** of His faith being challenged, and built up, and he had no idea. Keep reading, and you will see the **Process** unfold in the verses below, *Mark 5:30-33.*

30. *"And Jesus, immediately knowing in himself that virtue had gone out of him, turned him about in the press, and said, Who touched my clothes?"*

31. *"And his disciples said unto him, Thou seest the multitude thronging thee, and sayest thou, Who touched me?"* **JAIRUS WAITING IN THE PROCESS.**

32. *"And he looked round about to see her that had done this thing."* **JAIRUS WAITING IN THE PROCESS.**

33. *"But the woman fearing and trembling, knowing what was done in her, came and fell down before him, and told him all the truth."* **JAIRUS WAITING IN THE PROCESS.**

34. *"And he said unto her, Daughter, thy faith hath made thee whole; go in peace, and be whole of thy plague."* <u>JAIRUS WAITING IN THE PROCESS.</u>

Jesus rewarded her faith in Him by healing her body. It is her kind of amazing faith that we must operate in, step out on, and hold onto in the midst of whatever the circumstances look like. We must take advantage of the lesson being taught here. We must learn how to **Believe God**.

That powerful example of believing God reaped great rewards for the woman with the issue of blood. But let's travel a little further down the road with Jesus and Jairus as they journey to Jairus' house. Yes, God performed a miracle for this woman along the path. Wait, just wait and see what the synagogue ruler will have to believe Jesus for. The power of God is so awesome!

Now imagine how anxious and concerned, even nervous, Jairus had to be. His daughter was very ill, at the point of death, and he'd sought out Jesus to ask Him to come and help his daughter. Now he didn't send a servant or someone else. He traveled to seek out Jesus and personally ask Him to lay hands on his child. Jesus agreed to go with him but stopped along the way to talk with a woman who hadn't asked Him for anything. She hadn't even spoken to Jesus, while the ruler of the synagogue's daughter was dying and he had personally asked for Jesus' help.

Look deeper here at this teaching moment, which Jesus was utilizing to do two very specific things.

1. Jesus needed to show that all power was in His hands. He alone was able to heal naturally and spiritually. To show this beyond a shadow of doubt would nurture the seed of **Faith** and cause **Faith** to grow in who Jesus was and what He said.
2. And Jesus was walking in obedience to God the Father with the knowledge and purpose that all He did would glorify God.

Throughout Jesus' encounter with this woman, Jairus was in the process. **What was the process?** The process entailed Jairus learning to wait on Jesus to bless him by healing his daughter. He had to wait for that healing while Jesus healed someone else right in front of him. God works on His timetable and not ours. Because we have to wait for a blessing to be manifested in our lives doesn't necessarily mean the blessing is not coming. We must trust God and understand that He knows the right time to bless us. He knows what is best for us, because He knows our beginning, everything that will happen in the middle as we travel through life, and He surely knows our end. That just means He is equipped to bless us, He knows when to bless us, and He knows if what we want is truly the best thing for us. The Bible says, *"Blessed is that man that maketh the LORD his trust…" Psalm 40:4.*

The process was the synagogue ruler's faith in Jesus' healing power <u>being proven to him</u> by the healing of the woman with the issue of blood. But the process didn't stop there, because Jesus would take Jairus' faith to the next level. He would take it to a level beyond his ability to even think possible. The Bible assures us of it. *"Now unto him that is able to do exceeding abundantly above all that we ask or think, according to the power that worketh in us," Ephesians 3:20.*

The process was the <u>stretching of Jairus' faith and his ability to hold onto that faith in Jesus even in the face of fear and uncertainty. And not letting go of that faith, even when God is silent.</u> Jesus stopped on the journey to Jairus' home; he was quiet regarding Jairus' request because He was helping someone else. Jairus might have wanted to say to Jesus, "Lord, please hurry. My child is dying. This woman can wait. My child needs you, right now." This concerned and fearful father didn't realize that Jesus was using his circumstances to build his faith in an all-powerful God. Jesus would show him that He can meet our needs no matter how great. Our job is to trust Him past what we see.

ARE YOU IN THE PROCESS?

Learning how to **Believe God** is a process. Things happen in our lives that we do not understand. Those things, whether they are (tragedies, challenges, sickness, even death) as hard as it may be to believe, can serve an impactful purpose. Growing in our faith can take time, and it definitely is a **Process**. When I say **Process** – I mean, we don't typically start out on our faith walk with God having <u>**Mega Faith**</u>. Our ability to have faith in God, trust Him beyond what we can see, believe, and even understand, that is a process. We have to grow to that level of faith – that <u>**Mega Faith**</u>.

Jairus was on his journey toward <u>**Mega Faith**</u> and didn't even know it. The process for him to learn how to grow in his faith had already begun. We know that he had a measure of faith, because he sought out Jesus for help.

The process of growing in faith becomes strikingly clear in this passage of scripture. *"While he yet spake, there came from the ruler of the synagogue's house certain which said, Thy daughter is dead: why troublest thou the Master any further?" Mark 5:35.*

"As soon as Jesus heard the word that was spoken, he saith unto the ruler of the synagogue, <u>Be not afraid, only believe</u>," Mark 5:36.

So this was the end for the little girl, according to the person who made the proclamation to Jairus that his daughter was dead. In the natural realm, this would have been the end. Typically, dead means there is no hope for any other outcome; stop; give up. It's over!

Death was not the end for the little girl. Why? Because Jesus declared death was not the end for her. Jesus continued the journey to the ruler's home. There He found those weeping and filled with grief and great sorrow. But death and grief could not hinder the power of Jesus.

The Bible proclaims, **"And when he was come in, he saith unto them, 'Why make ye this ado, and weep? The damsel is not dead, but sleepeth.' And they laughed him to scorn. But when he had put them all out, he taketh the father and the mother of the damsel, and them that were with him, and entereth in where the damsel was lying. And he took the damsel by the hands, and said unto her, Talitha cu-mi: which is, being interpreted, Damsel, I say unto thee, arise,"** Mark 5:39-41.

"And straightway the damsel arose, and walked; for she was of the age of twelve years. And they were astonished with a great astonishment," Mark 5:42.

<u>Point of Grace</u> - The miracle working power of Jesus here shows us that He is in control. Not the world, not doctors, nothing, and no one is more powerful than our Lord and Savior. Now what I don't want

you to miss is the fact that Jesus put those that laughed Him to scorn out of the house before He worked the miracle. Why? He put them out because, **They Did Not Believe! So I say to you again, Only Believe!**

Hold onto this – In the midst of you learning to have faith in God, remember there is a **Process**. That process consists of the below things:

1. Take your request to the Lord in prayer.
2. Wait for God's answer.
3. Trust that God knows what is best for you.
4. In the process, you may get some bad news. You may see other people being blessed while you are still waiting for your blessing. Your prayer may not be answered as quickly as you want. That's okay. **ONLY BELIEVE!** Even when God is silent and anxiety or fear starts to attack you, look past what you see, trust the *Word* and promises of God, and **ONLY BELIEVE!**

Trust God even when He is silent, and circumstances make you wonder if your blessing is on the way, especially when you see other people being blessed. Those are times when you need to trust that God is ruling in your life. You're in the process. God is teaching you how to grow in your faith and ability to trust Him. This is when we learn to wait and see God move and show Himself true to His *Word*. Learn to trust that your blessings are on the way and keep it moving in Jesus. Don't doubt the love of God just because you feel like your blessing is slow in coming. Or you start to feel unsure that it is coming at all. Maybe God is quiet. Quiet or not, God's love is real, and it is faithful.

What is God's Quiet Love? I grew up in a household where there was quiet love. My mom hardly ever said I love you. Nor did my siblings and I grow up saying I love you to each other. But my mother's children knew there was nothing she wouldn't do for us. If her children got into trouble and needed to be bailed out of jail, or fell on hard times and needed money, my mom would do whatever she had to do to get her children out of trouble.

It was the same way with my brothers. If a fight broke out and one of my brothers was involved, you better believe every one of them was going to jump in the fight to take up for the other one. Our household didn't have a lot of what I called a kissy, kissy love, but we had deep love that we displayed by helping one another. Remember, when God is quiet, His love is still in full effect.

Remember the *Word* in *Zephaniah 3:17,* *"The Lord your God is in your midst, A victorious warrior. He will exult over you with joy, He will be quiet in His love, He will rejoice over you with shouts of joy."* Jesus was very well aware of everything that was happening in Jairus' life during the process. When the men from his house came and announced that Jairus' daughter was dead and asked why he was still troubling the master, Jesus spoke boldly and said to Jairus, **"Only Believe."**

Often God has to take us through something or allow something to happen that gives Him the opportunity to show us who He is. Perfect example, God used the children of Israel's forty-year wilderness experience to show them He is God Almighty; He could provide for them even in the wilderness. He could protect them; He could love them and forgive them when they sinned. Read the *16th chapter of Exodus* and see how God provided for Israel in the wilderness. They faced many challenges, hard things, fearful things, but that was part of the process needed for God to show them that He was a dependable God, and they could have faith in Him.

It is the same God of Israel that loves us and will reveal Himself to us as we go through the process of building our faith. And when we get to the other side, which is where **Faith** resides abundantly, it is then that you can see God clearly. You can look past that mountain of misery in your life, that pit of pain, and yes, that world of worry that we live in, which threatens to consume us daily. It is then that we can see that our God is capable to do absolutely anything.

SAY IT WITH ME, "BELIEVE GOD IN THE PROCESS."
<u>Allow me to share a brief testimony to the glory of God.</u>

Several years ago, my husband, Pastor Larry, went to Webster Middle School to vote. He wanted to move our church service there because the school had a nice auditorium. The auditorium was available for us to use. However, the engineer told my husband there was no storage space available to store our equipment after our church service.

I fell on my face before the Lord in prayer and began to seek Him. About two hours later, my husband called and told me that he had spoken to the engineer at the school again, and there was indeed storage space available for us. I'm not sure what happened, but God made it possible for us to move our service into Webster Middle School through the power of prayer.

My prayer for you is that you will take the measure of faith given to you by God <u>into custody and remain firm</u>, with strong faith, despite what you see, until what you need to believe God for manifests itself in the natural.

God has given each of us a measure of faith. *Romans 12:3, "For through the grace given to me I say to every one among you not to think* more highly of himself than he ought to think; but to think so as to have sound judgment, as God has allotted to each a measure of faith."

Prayer - Lord, You are true to Your *Word*. Help me to <u>**Only Believe,**</u> no matter what I see. In times of trouble, help me to hold onto memories of the many times that You have made a way for me. When You are working in my life, I want to be able to let go and allow You to be in control of the <u>**Process**</u> as I learn to grow in my faith walk. I want to have <u>**Mega Faith**</u>. I want to <u>**Only Believe**</u>. In Jesus Name, Amen!

I am enjoying our walk through this book,
and I am encouraged by all that God planted
in my spirit to share with you.
Know that His *Word* is rich and true.
"Jesus said unto him, If thou canst believe, all things are possible to him that believeth," Mark 9:23.

CHAPTER FOUR

I Believe Even When He Is Quiet

When the storms of life are raging, and the winds of adversity threaten to move my feet from that firmly planted place in God, I hold onto and refuse to let go of the only sure thing I know in this world that will never change, God.

I believe God's *Word* and His rich promises. The Bible is filled with promises of healing, deliverance, long life, salvation, financial prosperity, spiritual gifts, and blessings overflowing. God even promises us eternal life. *"Jesus said unto her, I am the resurrection, and the life: he that believeth in me, though he were dead, yet shall he live: And whosoever liveth and believeth in me shall never die. Believest thou this?" John 11:25-26.*

God said it! So I believe it! Not only am I promised eternal life with God, but I can expect life more abundantly even in this sometimes cruel and evil world. The Bible tells us, *"The thief cometh not, but for to steal, and to kill, and to destroy: I am come that they might have life, and that they might have it more abundantly," John 10:10.*

I believe that. Here's why!

It is God's desire to bless us, care for us, protect us, and meet our needs. Yet there are times when God is silent. During those times of silence, we must stand on our faith in Him. We must continue to believe His promises and not let doubt and fear crumble the foundation of our belief in God and His *Word*. Let's examine the powerful account of God's silence as Job endured tragic losses, sorrow, and physical affliction, *Job 1:13-22*.

All of Job's children were killed at the same time, his wealth of animals, servants, and his house were also destroyed. As he endured all that had come against him, Job's body was clothed with painful sores and worms that tormented him. He was unable to even find sleep in order to escape the pain that plagued his body, *Job 7:4-5*.

In the midst of all of this, God was silent. Who can trust and continue to believe God during such a whirlwind of death, calamity, and physical pain? Could you bear such tragedy and continue to trust and believe God? Job did just that! Let's consider the actions of God's servant Job.

Job felt the silence of God, and he said, *"Oh that I knew where I might find him! That I might come even to his seat! I would order my cause before him, and fill my mouth with arguments," Job 23:3-4.*

Job continued to speak what was in his heart. *"Behold, I go forward, but he is not there; and backward, but I cannot perceive him: On the left hand, where he doth work, but I cannot behold him:*

he hideth himself on the right hand that I cannot see him: But he knoweth the way that I take: when he hath tried me, I shall come forth as gold. My foot hath held his steps, his way have I kept, and not declined. Neither have I gone back from the commandment of his lips; I have esteemed the words of the Lord more than my necessary food," Job 23:8-12.

I am so encouraged by the steadfast mindset and heart of Job. Through everything that happened to him, at every turn, Job remained steadfast and un-moveable in his belief in God, faith, and trust in Him. Even in God's silence, Job did not stop believing God or trusting His *Word*. Job said that his foot had not slipped, meaning that he continued to walk with God according to His *Word*. He was determined to continue to obey God's commandments. And he confessed how much the *Word* of God meant to him; it meant more than the necessary food required to sustain his body.

God is a God of restoration. He can restore us <u>Spiritually</u> and naturally. God restored Job because Job held onto God and continued to believe God and spoke well of God amid all his pain and sorrow. God blessed Job with more children, more livestock, and even more wealth than he had in the beginning. *"So the Lord blessed the latter end of Job more than his beginning for he had fourteen thousand sheep, and six thousand camels, and a thousand yoke of oxen, and a thousand she asses. He had also seven sons and three daughters," Job 42:12-13.*

But that is not all God did for Job. *"And in all the land were no women found so fair as the daughters of Job: and their father gave them inheritance among their brethren. After this lived Job an hundred and forty years, and saw his sons, and his sons' sons, even four generations. So Job died, being old and full of days," Job 42:15-17.*

Wow! The restoration power of God is incredible. We know that things are not always going to work out the way we plan or the way we need. The waters of life toss us to and fro sometimes. That is just the reality that we are all bound to experience at some point. Yet we can choose to **Believe God** and hold onto our faith in Him. It is our faith that will equip and enable us to stay the predestined course in life that God has plotted out for us.

Point of Grace - Let's keep in mind that it doesn't matter what you see. That's right! What you see in the natural is irrelevant. What matters is what God says. *"While we look not at the things which are seen, but at the things which are not seen: for the things which are seen are temporal; but the things which are not seen are eternal,"* 2nd *Corinthians 4:18.* It does not matter what you see, because we need to hold onto our faith in God, who is eternal and all-powerful. And without faith, it is impossible to please God. He makes that very clear in His *Word*.

"And <u>without faith it is impossible to please God</u>, because anyone who comes to him must <u>believe that he exists</u> and that <u>he rewards those who earnestly seek him</u>," Hebrews 11:6.

One last point that I want to make about Job, we don't always have to be in sin for bad things to happen to us. Job had not sinned. His three friends Eliphaz, Bildad, and Zophar believed that he had sinned against God and challenged him to admit that he was in error. God is a sovereign God. That means He can do as He will. He can bless us; He can protect us, and even allow us to be tried. And that was the case with Job. God allowed Job to be tried.

However, just like Job said in the *23rd chapter*, *"When he hath tried me, I shall come forth as gold."*

When you are being tested, trials and tribulations press down hard upon you, will you stand the course, continue to **Believe God** and come forth as gold? Job's friends accused him of being guilty of sin, and that was why he was plagued with the tragedy that had come against him. In reality, Job had not sinned. God had simply allowed Satan to come against him because He knew that Job would not forsake Him in the midst of the storms raging in his life. God knew intimately the heart of Job, and He knew that Job would continue to believe in Him. God loves us, and in His time, He will break the silence and speak to us and work on our behalf.

When you have sinned, do you sometimes wonder if God hears your prayers?

You may have wondered if God answers the prayers of a sinner? Surely, that has been a question amongst Biblical theologians for centuries. The answer is a resounding, yes. I say that with confidence, since the Bible confirms it for me. Let's be realistic; no one is perfect. No one is without sin. However, we can strive toward perfection in Jesus Christ. *"For all have sinned, and come short of the glory of God," Romans 3:23.*

What do I do when God is silent? Great question! Let's talk about it.

When God is silent, you may feel uncertain, without direction, and a bit like you are standing on shaky ground. These feelings come over you because you start to think maybe God won't deliver you from your dilemma or solve your problem. Whatever it is, doubt begins to chip away at your ability to **Believe God**.

That silence can be frustrating and manifest into fear and make us stumble on our faith walk if we don't heed the *Word* of the Lord in our hearts.

1ˢᵗ Corinthians 15:58, "Therefore, my beloved brethren, be ye stedfast, unmoveable, always abounding in the work of the Lord, forasmuch as ye know that your labor is not in vain in the Lord."

When we do not hear the Lord's voice in our spirit, we need to remember that He is always speaking to us in His *Word*. There will always be a path for us to follow that is ordered by God. We just have to choose to use it. You've probably heard someone refer to the Bible as the (Basic Instruction Before Leaving Earth). That makes perfect sense to me. In order for me to go to heaven, I need to know how to get there.

But let's first talk about why God might be silent. Just because God is silent, it does not mean that He has forsaken you. When Jesus was preparing to go to the cross and die for the sins of mankind, He said, *"My God, my God, why hast thou forsaken me?" Matthew 27:46.*

God did not forsake Jesus, and He will not forsake you. Examine yourself to consider if you are playing a role in God's silence. You didn't expect me to say that, did you? Consider the below things:

1. Is there an un-confessed and un-repented sin that you need God's forgiveness for? *"If I had not confessed the sin in my heart, my Lord would not have listened," Psalm 66:18.* Search yourself; sometimes, we have to look deeper than what is on the surface. That lie you told and the foul language you use when you are angry are easy to identify. Search your heart and mind as well. Are your motives right? Is there someone or

something that you make more important than God? Have you forgiven those who may have hurt you, even if they did not ask you to forgive them? We should all consider these things when we want to hear from the Lord.

2. We must know and accept that God is a Sovereign God. He can do as He pleases, and He can move in our lives in His own time. When we choose to accept the sovereignty of God, we must trust and believe that He is all-powerful and all-knowing and that He is faithful to His ***Word***. Basically, you need to **Believe God**. Job knew that in his heart, and he understood the sovereignty of God. Though he had not sinned against God, yet tragedy had fallen upon him. He still refused to curse God as his foolish wife suggested. Read the exchange between Job and his wife in ***Job 2:9-10***. *"Then said his wife unto him, Dost thou still retain thine integrity? Curse God, and die. But he said unto her, Thou speakest as one of the foolish women speaketh. What? Shall we receive good at the hand of God, and shall we not receive evil? In all this did not Job sin with his lips."* Job was simply saying because He is God, He can do as He pleases. And still, I will trust Him.

3. Are you truly listening to God and willing to follow His directions? Sometimes God gives us the answer; it is just not the answer that we want. In those instances, we either continue to seek God for a different answer, or we attempt to do things on our own. Either path we take, we are not being receptive to what God has told us. And just like that disobedient child suffers the consequences of not following the instructions of their parents; there are times when we find

ourselves in the penalty box also. So sometimes, difficult things come our way out of disobedience, others come, and we must accept them as an opportunity to trust, lean on, and **Believe God** will see us through.

Allow me to share a personal testimony with you.

I had an assignment to speak at a service for Apostle James & Kimberly Sheets during their "Jesus Movement Conference," October 24, 2018. A terrible cold attacked my body. At the airport, I slammed my thumb in my husband's car door. Needless to say, it was painful. The attacks kept coming. While going through check-in at the airport, I became so weak that the Paramedics were called.

Twice, I was asked by the airport attendants, "Do you want to cancel your flight?" I refused. I knew Satan was attacking me to keep me from attending the conference and preaching the anointed *Word* God had given me for His people. Sickness and an injury to my thumb could not hinder me. I boarded that plane, pressed my way to the conference, and preached the *Life Changing Word* that God had put down inside me. Praise God!

There will be times in life that we must **Believe God** past what we see and how we feel. You will have natural battles in the flesh with sickness, fatigue etc. You will have battles in the Spiritual when you know God has called you to do something, and it will feel like the force of the universe is coming against you. Stand, be still, and know that He is God, *Psalm 46:10*.

In the next chapter, we will talk about prayer. It is our powerful mode of communication with the Lord. Don't stop reading. Join me in the next chapter, and I promise you will be encouraged.

Prayer - Precious and Righteous God, I pray that this book is encouraging and nourishing to someone who desires to know You. Only You can navigate the twists and turns in this life that are sure to shake our paths unless You guide us. In Jesus Name, Amen!

"Cast thy burden upon the LORD, and he shall sustain thee:
He shall never suffer the righteous to be moved."
Psalm 55:22

CHAPTER FIVE

I Believe God And The Power Of Prayer

Our **Belief in God** can manifest *Fruitful Prayers*. When we pray, we expect God to answer our prayers. Sometimes the answer does not come as quickly as we would like. Other times, we do not receive the answer we want. There are times when no answer comes at all. In order for us to experience a fruitful prayer life that results in answered prayers, the following three things are critical:

1. We must, beyond all doubt, accept in our heart, and believe in our soul, that God is God Almighty. There is no other source more powerful than Him. The *Word* of God says, *"Now unto Him that is able to do exceeding abundantly above all that we ask or think, according to the power that worketh in us,"* *Ephesians 3:20*. We must stand un-moveable, always

abounding in that fervent proclamation. We must pray with confidence that God has the power to do the very thing that we ask of Him.

2. It is also imperative we trust that God has great things for us and wants to bless us with them, to include the desires of our heart. God promises in His *Word*, *"For I know the thoughts that I think toward you, saith the Lord, thoughts of peace, and not evil, to give you an expected end," Jeremiah 29:11.* There is power in our ability to trust God and believe that He knows what is best for us.

3. We must learn to wait for the Good Hand of God to move in our lives. The plan that God has for our lives is not driven by our timeline. God's hand moves across the landscape of our lives at just the right moment. *"Be still and know that I am God," Psalm 46:10.* That is a powerful *Word* that God has spoken into our lives. We don't know the beginning and the end of things that shall transpire in our lives, but God does. If we wait on Him, we will be blessed.

<u>Point of Grace</u> - Prayer is so powerful. It is such an intimate connection to God. Your prayers and the life which you live before God can change the very heart of God. That statement might sound odd to you. However, it is absolutely true.

Consider King Hezekiah, who was the 13th king over Judah. He was a very righteous king who was obedient to God. His father, King Ahaz, was one of the worst kings in the history of Judah. He led the people of Israel astray with idolatry, allowing them to worship other gods.

Hezekiah was faithful to God, the one and only real God, the God of Israel. He reopened the temple in Jerusalem. He boldly sanctified the temple's vessels that were used to worship idol gods. This man of God restored the Levitical priest, which God had ordained as the only tribe, (Levi), which could hold the office of a priest, ***Deuteronomy 18:1-5***. Hezekiah also restored proper worship before God. This king loved God and was wholeheartedly committed to serving God and requiring the same of the people of Judah. Restoring the priest was an important step in purifying the temple. You can read more details in 2nd **Chronicles 29-32**.

The *Word* of God tells us in *2nd Kings 18:5*, *"He trusted in the Lord God of Israel; so that after him was none like him among all the kings of Judah, nor any that were before him."*

As you continue to read, you will find in *2nd Kings 20:1*, Hezekiah was sick unto death. The prophet Isaiah went to the king and said, *"...Thus saith the Lord, Set thine house in order; for thou shalt die, and not live."* But Hezekiah did not let those words shake his foundational trust in the God that he served. He turned his face to the wall and cried out to the God that he had so faithfully served. From the bowels of his soul, Hezekiah cried out in *2nd Kings 20:3*, *"I beseech thee, O LORD, remember now how I have walked before thee in truth and perfect heart, and have done that which is good in thy sight."* The *Word* says, *"Hezekiah wept sore."*

God's heart changed toward the plan that He had for Hezekiah. The decree of death would not be the last word God had for Hezekiah. I am so moved by this account that shows God's love and how our prayers and the life we live before Him can change the mind and heart of God. In verses 4-6, it reads, *"And it came to pass, afore Isaiah was gone out into the middle court, that the Word of the LORD came to him, saying, Turn again, and tell Hezekiah the captain of my people, Thus saith the LORD, the God of David thy father, I have heard thy prayer. I have seen thy tears, behold, I will heal thee: on the third day thou shalt go up unto the house of the LORD. And I will add unto thy days fifteen years; and I will deliver thee and this city out of the hand of Assyria; and I will defend this city for mine own sake, and for my servant David's sake."*

What a remarkable and encouraging testament to the power of prayer. God's *Word* tells us that, "*...The effectual fervent prayer of a righteous man availeth much," James 5:16.* We must cultivate a relationship with God that is infused by a need and desire to be connected to Him. That relationship will grow and mature because of righteous living. We then surrender our effectual fervent prayers unto a loving God, who is able to give us an expectant and expedient end.

Maybe you haven't spent a lot of time praying. Perhaps, you feel like you're not real sure exactly how to pray. No problem! Prayer is simply your opportunity to speak your heart to God. You can tell Him your fears, what you need Him to do for you, ask Him to help you make a decision that you are struggling with, bless your family, keep your children safe, heal your body, and even ask Him for something that most of us need. Yes, you can ask God to bless your finances.

But before we start asking God for what we need or want from Him, we need to thank God for all of His many blessings. When we pray, let's remember to include the below things:

1. Praise God just for being God. Exalt Him! Give Him honor and worship Him because He is so wonderful, loving, and such

a forgiving God. Tell Him how much you love Him and want your life to be pleasing unto Him.

2. Next, thank God for all of His wonderful blessings. Thank God for His goodness and mercy, and how He has blessed you and made a way for you when you know that no one else could have done that specific thing for you, but God.

3. You need to remember to repent before the Lord. Ask God to forgive you for any sins that you know you have committed. Big or small, sin is sin. God wants you to repent of those sins, because He wants to forgive you. Even the great warrior David, who became King David, knew how to repent. *"Have mercy upon me, O God, According to Your loving kindness; According to the multitude of Your tender mercies, Blot out my transgressions," Psalm 51:1.* It is just that simple; you just sincerely say, "Lord forgive me."

4. Now, go ahead and ask God for what you need Him to do for you. Ask Him for that thing you need Him to fix or bring to pass. You can trust that God wants great things for you. He wants us to come to Him in prayer. This verse encourages us to do just that. *"Be anxious for nothing, but in everything by prayer and supplication, with thanksgiving, let your requests be made known to God." Philippians 4:6.*

5. Remember prayer is your time to communicate with God. And like any communication, it is a two-way street. So linger in prayer for a little while. Once you have talked to God and given Him your petition, wait. Yes, wait for God to speak to you. Allow Him time to give you the peace that you needed when you went to Him in prayer in the first place. Allow Him to

speak to your heart and soul and give you the answer that you need. Prayer helps us to feel close to God. We can leave the presence of God feeling encouraged and lighter because we've left our heavy burdens with Him. We feel strengthened and able to keep pressing forward, trusting that God will answer our prayer and take good care of us.

6. Now that you have prayed and even waited for God to speak to you, walk away with faith that God can do all things. So surely He can do that little or big thing that you have asked of Him. Let's close our prayer by saying, "In Jesus Name, Amen." Jesus tells us to do just that. *St. John 14:13-14, "And whatsoever ye shall ask in my name, that will I do, that the Father may be glorified in the Son. If ye shall ask anything in my name, I will do it."*

The Power of Prayer is strong, and <u>**I Believe God**</u> and His *Word*. *"Rejoice always, pray without ceasing, in everything give thanks; for this is the will of God in Christ Jesus for you," 1st Thessalonians 5:16-17.* Yes, God counsels us to pray.

So the next time you feel unsure, worried, lonely, or unloved, don't know which way to turn, you have no resolution for the problem that feels too heavy for you to carry, go to God in prayer. I promise that He will meet you there. He is truly a problem solver; the best that there is. He loves you, and He will be there for you. Just give God a chance. *"So let us come boldly to the throne of our gracious God. There we will receive his mercy, and we will find grace to help us when we need it," Hebrews 4:16.*

Prayer - Lord, You are a wonderful, loving and righteous God. You deserve to be praised, and I bow down with my heart and soul to worship You. Please forgive me of my sins. I desire to be right in Your eyes. Thank You for all of Your many blessings, great and small. Father, help me to boldly come to You with all faith that You know what is best for me. Help me to seek Your guidance in all things. Help me to be who You desire for me to be.

In Jesus Name, Amen!

CHAPTER SIX-A
Train Your Human Spirit To Believe God

"For it is with your heart that you believe and are justified, and it is with your mouth that you profess your faith and are saved," Romans 10:10.

The word heart in the above scripture is not referring to our human physical heart. Not our heart that is the vital organ in our chest cavity that pumps blood. The word heart in our scripture is referring to our human spirit; **"the inner self"** or spirit. We believe God with our human spirit. Let's hold onto that proclamation as we examine this chapter.

In chapter three, we learned that man is a three-part being, (spirit, soul and body). *1st Thessalonians 5:23* teaches us that man's spirit or human spirit is the real you. *Genesis 2:7* teaches that the breath that God breathed into Adam's nostrils is the human spirit. In chapter two, we established that it is through the human spirit that God communicates with us, which is how we receive from God, *Proverbs 20:27*. It is also how we establish and build a growing relationship with God while we learn to believe and trust Him, *Job 32:8*.

The moment we believe in Jesus as our Lord and Savior, our human spirit is instantaneously born again. Our human spirit is made alive. It is then that God's Holy Spirit can live within our human spirit and transform our minds, lives, and actions, causing us to be like Christ. The renewing of our mind is critical for us to be like Christ and have the mind of Christ. To what then is our mind renewed to? Great question! You are thinking and considering what is being said here. *Philippians 2:5* answers that question for us. *"Let this mind be in you, which was also in Christ Jesus."* God's *Word* clearly says that we need to have the mind of Jesus.

When we have the mind of Christ, we can then separate ourselves from the sin and insanity that the world welcomes with open arms. By the power of God's Holy Spirit, we can walk in the newness of life with a renewed mind and a changed character that grows to be like Christ. That is a process that takes time and diligence as we walk with Christ, and patiently wait for His loving guidance.

"And be not conformed to this world: but be ye transformed by the renewing of your mind, that ye may prove what is that good, and acceptable, perfect will of God," Romans 12:2.

What a powerful directive given to us by the *Word* of God in *Romans 12:2*. It is not by our own verbal proclamation or simply joining a church that we become a Christian. But it is by the powerful life changing Holy Spirit of God, <u>which transforms our mind, our actions, and our lives.</u> It is then that the human spirit can be trained by your renewed mind to **Believe God**. It can be trained to believe Him for a difficult thing, trained to believe Him past what you see. Yes, trained to believe and accept that God is all-powerful, and able to do all things. Our mind and heart willingly accepts the Bible as God's *Word* and the path to righteousness and eternal life with God. *"But ye are not in the flesh, but in the Spirit, if so be that the Spirit of God dwell in you. Now if any man have not the Spirit of Christ, he is none of his." Romans 8:9.*

The Bible tells us in the born again experience our human spirit is born again from the incorruptible seed of God, and restored back into fellowship with God through the everlasting *Word* of God, which dwells in our human spirit forever and is renewed daily. Consider the below three verses. Do you notice anything that stands out about the verse with Jesus speaking to Nicodemus?

- *1ˢᵗ Peter 1:23, "Having been born again, not of corruptible seed but incorruptible, through the word of God which lives and abides forever."*

- *2ⁿᵈ Timothy 4:22, "The Lord be with your spirit. Grace be with you all."*

- Nicodemus, who was a ruler of the Jews, went to Jesus by night. Jesus had made a proclamation in *John 3:3* that man would have to be born again in order to see the Kingdom of God. Confused, Nicodemus asked Jesus how that could be possible when a man was old. Here is the good part, Jesus answered him saying, *"Verily, verily, I say unto thee, Except a man be born of the water and the Spirit, he cannot enter into the Kingdom of God. That which is born of the flesh is flesh; and that which is born of the Spirit is spirit,"* John 3:5-6.

Notice the words "Spirit and spirit" in the scripture above when Jesus spoke to Nicodemus. The first word **Spirit** is capitalized and refers to the Spirit of God Almighty. The second word **spirit** is in lower case and refers to our human spirit. Man's human spirit needs to be born from above by God's Spirit. In the born again experience, it's our human spirit that believes in Jesus as our Savior and receives new birth by God's Spirit. Likewise, it is with our born again human spirit that we believe God to receive the supernatural throughout our Christian journey.

After the born again experience, the human spirit has to be trained how to believe God. Think about it this way, before we were saved our belief system and our moral gauge for right and wrong was driven by what our parent's taught us, and by the world's view or society at large. We naturally walked in fear, wearing it like a cloak, which could magically protect us if we just embraced it. And because science had no tangible proof that a God who is all-powerful and has no limitations could exist, the world trained our natural mind to question the belief of such a God. That's the reason why many churches immediately have "New Believers" classes for new converts.

These classes help renew the mind. They do so by introducing the following topics:

1. Knowing who you are in Christ.
2. The benefits in walking with Christ.

3. How to become more spiritually conscious of the things of the Spirit.

Some believers have been saved for many years and were taught church fundamentals, such as God can make a difference in your life, church attendance is essential for growing in God, trust God etc. However, they were taught little about how to train their human spirit to believe God for the supernatural. Or they were taught but lack the discipline it takes to develop the born again human spirit.

Without another level of understanding they are missing out on so much more that God has for them, through Jesus Christ. Let's consider the needed steps to train the human spirit to **<u>Believe God</u>**.

Step 1 - Exercise Being Sensitive to the Holy Spirit
1ˢᵗ Thessalonians 5:19, "Do not quench the Spirit."
Ephesians 4:30, "And do not grieve the Holy Spirit of God."

What does it mean to grieve or quench the Holy Spirit? The word **grieve**, which is used in the scripture above, means to sadden the Holy Spirit. The word **quench**, used above, means to extinguish or suppress the influence of the Holy Spirit.

There are several ways to grieve or sadden the Holy Spirit:

1. Not walking in love.
2. Not listening to the voice of the Holy Spirit.
3. Not believing the power of the *Word* of God.

These are just a few key ways to grieve the Holy Spirit. There are many other ways. Whenever the Holy Spirit speaks to our human spirit, it's vital that we be sensitive, and respond in obedience, because the Holy Spirit has personality and emotions. By the power of Jesus Christ, the Holy Spirit is our personal helper. *"And I will ask the Father, and he will give you another advocate to help you and be with you forever," John 14:16.* The Holy Spirit is that advocate.

It is a spiritual fire that dwells inside you. It directs and counsels you by nudging at you to do right. It is the quiet inner spiritual voice that speaks to you when sin is in your path and it tells you, "No, don't do it." And it nags at your heart and mind in the form of guilt and unrest when you are disobedient to that inner spiritual voice of counsel. It is detrimental to us to grieve the Holy Spirit. We should want to welcome God's connection to us. And allow the Holy Spirit to keep us close to God, and help us to navigate the twists and turns while traveling the path of this thing called life. God's Holy Spirit educates our human spirit about Him. It is that spiritually learned knowledge of God that causes our faith to grow and enables us to **Believe God**.

"These are the things God has revealed to us by his Spirit. The Spirit searches all things, even the deep things of God. For who knows a person's thoughts except their own spirit within them? In the same way no one knows the thoughts of God except the Spirit of God," 1st *Corinthians 2:10-11*.

The Holy Spirit in connection with our human spirit acts as a consuming fire, *Hebrews 12:29*, which extinguishes doubt and unbelief as He tenderly guides us. We must be sensitive to His prompting, or we will miss His gentle voice and care. Many times the Holy Spirit will speak an inspirational word to our human spirit just when we need encouragement, reminding us of the promises of God or giving us an uplifting song right in our moment of desperation.

Years ago, I was sitting in church, and it was a time in my life when I was feeling lonely, sad, and friendless. All of a sudden, out of my human spirit, I heard the Holy Spirit say in a loving and kind voice, "I'm your friend." The Holy Spirit comforted my spirit, and peace washed over me. In that moment, God reminded me that He was my friend and that He loved me. This particular scripture is such a blessing. *"No longer do I call you servants, for the servant does not know what his master is doing; but I have called you friends, for all that I have heard from my Father I have made known to you," John 15:15.*

At that time, I was young in my Christian walk, and right away, I assumed what I'd heard was my own thoughts. I probably would have dismissed the thoughts, but thank God for the Holy Spirit, which knew exactly what I was thinking. The Holy Spirit acted as a personal helper and immediately gave the speaker at the church an unction. Now understand, the speaker did not know what I was feeling or thinking. The speaker said, "He's your friend," as she proclaimed the *Word* of God to the congregation. My spirit was enlightened. It was a joyous and confirming moment for me as a young believer. My human spirit heard and recognized the voice of God, and <u>my faith was increased</u>. You see, the Holy Spirit was teaching me how to train my human spirit to recognize the voice of God. I would have saddened the Holy Spirit if I stubbornly refused to hear such a confirming word of truth.

God enlightens us through our human spirit. *Proverbs 20:27* tells us, *"The human spirit is the lamp of the Lord that sheds light on one's inmost being."* What does inmost mean? It is important to understand that word. I am glad you are engaged and truly want an understanding of God's *Word*. Inmost is defined as being deepest within the self; one's innermost feelings. You see, God knows the deep and secret part of us that no one else does. He knows even that inner part of us that we are not always honest with ourselves about, which could be flaws in our character, hidden, and un-repented sin. It could even be our lack of time spent with God that we don't want to acknowledge as being an issue.

Being sensitive to the Holy Spirit allows the Holy Spirit to teach and guide our human spirit to understand all of the teachings of Jesus in the scriptures. One of the vital teachings in Jesus' ministry was faith. In *Matthew 8:23-27*, Jesus calmed the storm. Let's examine this miracle.

Matthew 8:23-27 "Then he got into the boat and his disciples followed him. Suddenly a furious storm came up on the lake, so that the waves swept over the boat. But Jesus was sleeping. The disciples went and woke him, saying, Lord, save us! We're going to drown! He replied, 'You of little faith, why are you so afraid?' Then he got up and rebuked the winds and the waves, and it was completely calm. The men were amazed and asked, What kind of man is this? Even the winds and the waves obey him!"

Before Jesus calmed the storm, in this same chapter, the disciples witnessed Jesus perform many miracles. Jesus, the great teacher, took them through boot camp training for their human spirit. The things they witnessed helped them to grow in faith. They witnessed Jesus heal a man who was plagued with leprosy. Read about that miracle in *Matthew 8:1-4*. He also healed the Centurion's paralyzed servant in *Matthew 8:5-13*. Jesus was seen doing a miracle healing for His disciple, Peter, whose mother-in-law was sick with a fever, *Matthew 8:14-17*.

When Christ disciples were in the midst of a raging storm, seemingly they had forgotten the power they witnessed Jesus demonstrate right before their eyes performing various miracles. Jesus rebuked His disciples saying, "You of little faith." I believe their unbelief saddened Jesus' heart because they doubted His divinity after witnessing many miracles prior to them being caught up in a raging storm. Jesus' same work is carried on through the work of the Holy Spirit. It's vital that we are sensitive to the Holy Spirit because the Holy Spirit will teach us and help us to train our human spirit how to believe God.

Step 2 - Praying in the Spirit

"But you, my friends, keep on building yourselves up on your most sacred faith. Pray in the power of the Holy Spirit," Jude 1:20.

As a young girl in my teens and living in project housing, we had an upstairs bedroom my mom converted into what we called the sitting room. It had living room furniture instead of bedroom furniture. Family members and anyone from the project housing complex, who wanted to be baptized in the Holy Spirit with evidence of speaking in tongues, were welcome. We would fast and go to the sitting room to pray and be filled with the Holy Spirit. Back in those days, a lot of emphases was placed on receiving the Holy Spirit with the evidence of speaking in tongues.

I remember seeking the Holy Spirit in our sitting room. As I prayed, suddenly, my language changed to an unknown tongue. The experience was so exciting, and I wanted to share what was happening to me. I hurried downstairs and told my mother. I yelled out, "Mama, I got the Holy Ghost." The Holy Ghost took over my tongue again. And that language, that I didn't understand, but rolled off my tongue fluently by the power of the Holy Ghost, claimed my mouth and authored my words. I rushed outside and continued speaking in tongues. I'm sure that the people who saw me thought I was insane. I didn't care. The experience was great! I didn't want the Spirit that had a hold of me to let go. My mom must have been embarrassed or thought people would think that I was strange. She said to me, "Sandra, get in the house."

The gift of tongues or praying in the Spirit is a great privilege and a blessing to the body of Christ. It is a spiritual exercise that builds the believer's spiritual muscles and helps enhance our spiritual senses. Below are more spiritual benefits of speaking in tongues by the power of the Holy Ghost.

When we speak in tongues, we are praying the Will of God as the Holy Spirit gives us what to say:

Acts 2:4 proclaims, "All of them were filled with the Holy Spirit and began to speak in other tongues as the Spirit enabled them." Read the book of Acts. It will help to establish a foundational understanding of speaking in tongues and so much more. This book gives us a direct understanding of how the church began. And you are able to read about the gift of the Holy Spirit and its mighty power and impact on people and the outpouring of the gift of tongues, and its connection to the Holy Spirit.

Did you know that the Holy Spirit connects with our human spirit to pray the right kind of prayers? God is so amazing, and the power of His Holy Spirit is without restrictions. That is why God is referred to as being omnipotent, meaning all-powerful.

There are times when we do not know what we ought to pray, but the Spirit himself intercedes for us through wordless groans. *Romans 8:26* tells us that God speaks to His people through tongues. *"Likewise the Spirit also helpeth our infirmities: for we know not what we should pray for as we ought: but the Spirit itself maketh intercession for us with groanings which cannot be uttered."* God's *Word* helps us to understand the gift of speaking in tongues. *"For one who speaks in a tongue speaks not to men but to God; for no one understands him, but he utters mysteries in the Spirit," 1st Corinthians 14:2.*

Praying in tongues brings about spiritual edification. It intensifies our prayers, strengthens, and charges our human spirit. When you pray in tongues, you are empowered to do so by the Holy Spirit. When you pray in tongues, you are yielding your own human spirit to God's Holy Spirit, and you can be on one accord in the realm of God's anointing as you commune with Him. This spiritual connection with the Holy Spirit nurtures and strengthens your spiritual life. You are empowered to stand against Satan when he dares to come against you. Praying in tongues enables you to enter into an intimate time of prayer, worship, and praise with the Lord. It is powerful. *1st Corinthians 14:4, "Anyone who speaks in a tongue edifies themselves..." Jude 20:25 says, "But ye, beloved, building up yourselves on your most holy faith, praying in the Holy Ghost."*

We must grow in our spirit in order to continue to stand and believe God throughout our Christian journey. When we pray in the spirit, the Holy Spirit prays for us and helps us to pray the right kind of prayers, and pray the Will of God. So if you are struggling with believing God in any area of your life, begin praying in the spirit more often. Build a frequent and strong prayer life. It is critical that you make time to pray and commune with God. In *Ephesians 6:18,* the Bible advises us to pray in the Spirit for spiritual edification and the building up of your faith.

"The Spirit also helps us in our weakness. We do not know what we ought to pray for, but the Spirit himself intercedes for us through

wordless groans. And he who searches our hearts knows the mind of the Spirit, because the Spirit intercedes for God's people in accordance with the will of God," Romans 8:26-27.*

"For if I pray in a tongue, my spirit prays, but my mind is unproductive [because it does not understand what my spirit is praying]." Please read and digest this verse found in *1st Corinthians 14:14 (AMP)*. In these verses, we can see the importance of God's Spirit.

Let's talk about praise for just a minute. When we are praying in the Spirit, it is a form of praise. The *Word* tells us, *"Let everything that has breath praise the Lord," Psalm 150:6.* We are commanded in this verse to praise the Lord. Something significant and supernatural happens when we praise the Lord. Blessings start to flow in our lives. Fear and unbelief dissipate, and our heart will overflow with thanksgiving and joy.

However, there are times when praising God can be a struggle. Maybe, you are frustrated or struggling with depression, you've become weary waiting on God's promises, or finding it difficult to believe God. There's a Hebrew word called yadah, which means "praise, give thanks, or confess."

God is glorified and pleased when we praise and give Him thanks for His greatness and confess His goodness with the fruit of our lips. *"For the Lord is great and greatly to be praised; He is to be feared above all gods," Psalm 96:4.* Even if it's a sacrifice of praise through Jesus, we must continually praise God. *"Through Jesus, therefore, let us continually offer to God a sacrifice of praise, the fruit of lips that openly profess his name," Hebrews 13:15.*

Praising God helps us to take our focus off of ourselves and fix our eyes on God, who is the only one that can help us. When our eyes are on God, our faith is activated. I remember once when I was in prayer, I was more focused on my problem, and it was a struggle to pray. The devil was really trying to keep me from praying by distracting my mind. However, I made up in my mind that I was going to praise God instead of focus on my problems. As I began to thank God, over and over again, with all my heart in a sacrificial manner, a change took place.

The next thing I remember was my spirit being in the air in the corner of my bedroom looking down at my physical body, still in a position of prayer, on my knees thanking God. My spirit was very aware of where I was in the natural. You see, praise moved me into another realm in the Spirit. Praising God elevated my human spirit to another realm. Our physical bodies will endure tests and trials in life, but in the Spirit, we can be free and live above the cares and worries in this world when we learn to praise the Lord.

"Rejoice in the Lord always. I will say it again: Rejoice! Let your gentleness be evident to all. The Lord is near. Do not be anxious about anything, but in every situation, by prayer and petition, with thanksgiving, present your requests to God. And the peace of God, which transcends all understanding, will guard your hearts and your minds in Christ Jesus," Philippians 4:4-7.

<u>Point of Grace</u> - Power is in your praise. We are speaking life and unbelief will flee when we praise God and tell Him how wonderful He is. Our faith is activated to believe God. We should desire to be filled with the Spirit if we want that truly intimate and anointed walk with Christ.

"Do not get drunk on wine, which leads to debauchery. Instead, be filled with the Spirit, speaking to one another with psalms, hymns, and songs from the Spirit. Sing and make music from your heart to the

Lord, always giving thanks to God the Father for everything, in the name of our Lord Jesus Christ,"* Ephesians 5:18-20.

Romans 12:2, wisely tells the believer to be filled with the Spirit and not live after the customs of this world, *"The person without the Spirit does not accept the things that come from the Spirit of God but considers them foolishness, and cannot understand them because they are discerned only through the Spirit,"* 1st Corinthians 2:14.

The Bible also tells us, *"Let the word of Christ dwell in you richly in all wisdom; teaching and admonishing one another in psalms and hymns and spiritual songs, singing with grace in your hearts to the Lord,"* Colossians 3:16.

Praise is one of the things that God desires from us. He created us to praise him. *Isaiah 43:7, "[Even] every one that is called by my name: for I have created him for my glory, I have formed him, yea, I have made him."* When we are obedient and adhere to the *Word* of God that is a form of praise. When we are singing songs and dancing in the Spirit and praying in tongues that is giving God praise. When our lives are governed by the Spirit of God, and our character mimics that of Christ, we are giving God praise, and that pleases Him.

I have covered quite a bit of information. I would like to give you a moment to digest what we have covered so far in this chapter, including the first and second steps to training your human spirit to believe God. We will discuss step three in the second portion of this chapter, which will be Chapter 6-B.

"If we live in the Spirit, let us also walk in the Spirit."
Galatians 5:25

Prayer - Wonderful and Great God, we thank You for Your insightful *Word* that guides us. Thank You for Your Holy Spirit that embraces and nurtures our human spirit that we might be able to grow our faith and trust in You. Lord, as we open the door to the second half of this chapter, open our minds and the eyes of our soul that our human spirit may become one with Your Holy Spirit.

In Jesus Name, Amen!

CHAPTER SIX-B
Train Your Human Spirit To Believe God

Now, we're ready to consider the third step to training your human spirit to Believe God.

Step 3 - Faith works in line with God's Word.

Our human spirit becomes more sensitive to the things of the Holy Spirit the more we are focused on our spirit man. God designed our human spirit that way. I used to wear my glasses about six hours or more a day to see things from a distance. Without my glasses, I found it difficult to read street signs. When I started wearing my glasses less frequently, I noticed my natural vision was becoming sharper around the house, and I was able to read large street signs without my glasses from a distance. Likewise, our human spirit will become sharper and believe God the more we practice using our faith based on the *Word* of God.

Faith works in line with God's *Word*. All the promises of God are already ours through the finished work of Jesus Christ because he died on the cross for our sins. His sacrifice on the cross gave us the opportunity for salvation, sanctification, grace, healing, deliverance, eternal life and so much more.

If what we believe God for lines up with His *Word*, that will help us build our faith in God. We can then receive the great things that belong to us through Jesus Christ. Many people do not receive answered prayers, because they are trying to train their spirit to believe God, while they operate outside of God's *Word*.

For example: If you are believing God for a home but lie about your income on the loan application in order to get the home, that's not faith in God's ability to bless you with the home. That is your attempt to manipulate the process by lying about your income.

If you are believing God for a new job but include untrue job experience on the application in order to enhance your resume, you are not acting in faith. You are being deceitful and acting outside of God's *Word*. You might get the job, but God wasn't in it. God does not work outside of His *Word*. Our faith works in partnership with God's *Word*. When we learn to trust God, and believe in our human spirit that beyond what we see, the Almighty God can do the impossible, that is the vein in which we see miracles happen when we pray.

The account of Peter walking on water in ***Matthew 14:22-31*** is amazing. I enjoy teaching about this account because it's a good example of what can happen when we line up our faith with the *Word* of God. Peter saw Jesus walking on water. He was afraid and yet intrigued. Let's read the exchange between Peter and Jesus.

"...Be of good cheer; it is I: be not afraid." And Peter answered him and said, Lord, if it be thou, bid me come unto thee on the water. So he said, 'Come.' And when Peter was come down out of the ship, he walked on the water to go to Jesus," Matthew 14:28-29.

The Bible said Peter stepped out of the boat based on the spoken word from Jesus, **"Come."** Think about it. Peter's human spirit heard Jesus call to him, he believed and took action, all based on a word from Jesus. It was not humanly possible. Peter was defying the laws of nature that restricted him from being able to walk on unstable water. It wasn't the human common sense that Peter was operating in when he stepped out on the water. Peter was operating with his spiritual senses when he trusted Jesus enough to step out on the water. When he reverted back to the use of his human common sense, it was then that he began to sink.

"Why did you doubt?" I am paraphrasing Jesus' interaction with Peter. "Why did you take your spiritual eyes off of my word, **'Come'** and revert back to your human senses that are filled with doubt and fear?" Peter doubted and began to sink, and we too will begin to sink when we doubt God. Faith doesn't work with common sense. Faith and common sense are totally opposites and operate on two different frequencies. Doubt and fear operate based on human senses and the limitations of the human mind. Faith operates based on our born again human spirit, which enables us to believe God, based on the limitless possibilities of a God that has no boundaries in the natural or the spiritual.

This takes me to my next point on how to train our human spirit to believe God. We must study and meditate on His *Word*. Learning how to believe God to receive His promises begin with cultivating a life in the *Word*. Make it your mission to behold the *Word* of God every day. Overload yourself with the *Word*. Study and Meditate on the Scriptures. *"Open my eyes, that I may behold wondrous things out of your law," Psalm 119:18.* Studying God's *Word* provides spiritual edification to educate your spirit that you might know God better. His *Word* also enables you to understand His divine Will. The more we develop a personal relationship with God through His *Word*, the more we are able to train our spirit to believe God.

The more you read the Bible, the more you will want to read it. It will cultivate within you a desire to have a closer walk with God. The more time you spend reading and studying the Bible, the easier it is to trust the *Word* of God and get closer to God. We begin to understand that there is nothing that God cannot do, and our human spirit can learn to believe God. *"For the Lord gives wisdom; from his mouth come knowledge and understanding," Proverbs 2:6.*

Train your spirit to hear God's Spirit through His *Word*. According to **Romans 10:17,** *"...Faith comes by hearing, and hearing by the Word of God."* When our spirit (the inward man) hears the *Word* of God, it is quickened to believe. As we read the *Word*, study, and hear the *Word* of God preached, its power impacts us. It penetrates our heart and mind. It empowers us to receive and believe the truth that it contains.

Anytime you need a miracle, you have to believe and stand firmly on God's promises. You must carefully follow the *Word* of God, and stay focused on a path of faith that God is able to do that which you have asked of Him. I call this "putting on the blinders." Blinders are small leather screens attached to a horse's bridle. The blinders prevent the horse from having a peripheral view and keep it from getting distracted by its surroundings. That's what we need to do as believers when we hear something contrary to the promises of God. We need to put on our faith blinders and stay focused on the *Word* of God. This is the only way our faith can grow. And that is how we can see our prayers answered.

The Bible admonishes us to steadfastly follow Christ in believing God. *Luke 9:62, "But Jesus said to him, No one, having put his hand to the plow and looking back, is fit for the kingdom of God."* You began your Christian walk by accepting Christ as your Lord and Savior by faith. It is by faith and believing God's *Word* that we are able to successfully continue to flourish as a Christian. You believed God unto salvation, believe Him for your healing, financial blessings, peace, your marriage, and spiritual growth. Believe Him for all things.

We are not to swerve to the left or right from the path God's *Word* has carved out for us according to *Joshua 1:7*. Have you ever wondered why the straight path is so narrow? It is designed that way, so there is not enough room for you to stand still in idleness, nor turn around. Your purpose on the straight and narrow is to continually mature spiritually by faith through believing God. Remember, Jesus teaches us that anyone who starts out as a Christian believer but walks away from his faith is not worthy of the kingdom of God. We are to believe God for as long as we reside on this earth, and we accomplish this by staying focused.

The Bible offers Joshua an example of the importance of adhering to God's counsel. After Moses' death, his successor, Joshua, was installed as the leader. God said to Joshua, and I paraphrase, "Put on the faith blinders and carefully follow every word of My law. Do not turn aside to look to the left or right, but only stay focused." *Joshua 1:1-7* is a clear indication of why you must continually hear and carefully obey all of God's *Word*. Your faith grows when you continually hear and obey the *Word* of God.

An example of how the believer should respond when facing a challenge or negative report is found in the book of *Numbers, chapter 13*. Some men of Israel were sent to explore the land of Canaan, and some returned with an evil report. *Numbers 13:1-2, "And the Lord spoke to Moses, saying, Send men to spy out the land of Canaan, which I am giving to the children of Israel; from each tribe of their fathers you shall send a man, everyone a leader among them."*

Numbers 13:26-33, "Now they departed and came back to Moses and Aaron and all the congregation of the children of Israel in the Wilderness of Paran, at Kadesh; they brought back word to them and to all the congregation, and showed them the fruit of the land. Then they told him, and said: We went to the land where you sent us. It truly flows with milk and honey and this is its fruit. Nevertheless the people who dwell in the land are strong; the cities are fortified and very large; moreover we saw the descendants of Anak there. The Amalekites dwell in the land of the South; the Hittites, the Jebusites, and the Amorites dwell in the mountains; and the Canaanites dwell by the sea and along the banks of the Jordan." So spies gave their report of all they had seen.

Verses 30-33 continue by saying, "And Caleb stilled the people before Moses, and said, Let us go up at once, and possess it; for we are well able to overcome it. But the men that went up with him said, We be not able to go up against the people; for they are stronger than we. And they brought up an evil report of the land which they had searched unto the children of Israel, saying, The land, through which we have gone to search it, is a land that eateth up the inhabitants thereof; and all the people that we saw in it are men of a great stature. And there we saw the giants, the sons of Anak, which come of the giants: and we were in our own sight as grasshoppers, and so we were in their sight."

The leaders of Israel apparently missed what God said to Moses in *Numbers 13:2*. God said, *"Send some men to explore the land of Canaan, which I am giving to the Israelites…"* God wanted them to trust what He promised. He had already given them the land and saw them possessing it.

The evil report in the *Numbers chapter 13* account was so filled with doubt that it spread like wild fire among the people, contaminating their faith. It caused the people to worry, become agitated, fearful, and doubt the power of God. An evil report will cloud your thinking and cause you to forget everything God has said in His *Word*. When this happens, we have to remind ourselves, repeatedly, of what God has said in the Bible and only believe.

Whether you're dealing with an evil report or one of life's many challenges, the believer's <u>faith blinders</u> function to help us keep our focus straight ahead, on God. Regardless of what we see, feel, or hear, just as a horse's blinders are designed large enough to cover their eyes, the believer's <u>faith blinders</u> are designed to guard against what they hear. What we hear will either grow our faith and enable us to believe God's promises, or discourage our faith and produce fear and unbelief. Use your faith to protect yourself against anything that speaks against the wisdom and knowledge of God's *Word*.

Mark 4:24, *"Take heed what you hear…"* Apostle Paul counsels us in *2nd Corinthians 10:5*, *"Casting down imaginations, and every high thing that exalteth itself against the knowledge of God, and bringing into captivity every thought to the obedience of Christ."* We must carefully monitor what we hear and control our thoughts.

Anything we hear contrary to God's *Word* will breed unbelief. If faith comes by hearing and hearing by the *Word* of God according to ***Romans 10:17***, then certainly fear and doubt come by hearing words contrary to the Holy Bible.

The more you entreat the *Word* of God, the more natural it will become for you to respond to life's circumstances according to the *Word*. In order to entreat the *Word*, we need to read the *Word* daily, pray for God to give us an understanding of His *Word*, and not just read it, but allow it to speak to us. So hear the *Word* with your heart as well as your mind, and applying God's *Word* to your life will become fulfilling and your desire.

Keep the *Word* on your lips. Keep speaking the *Word* of God into your situations until what you are believing God for manifests itself in the natural. *"Death and life are in the power of the tongue: and they that love it shall eat the fruit thereof, Proverbs 18:21."* Don't allow negative words to come out of your mouth. Load your mouth with the powerful *Word* of God. Jesus made a profound proclamation in ***Mark 11:23-24***. *"Truly I tell you, if anyone says to this mountain, Go, throw yourself into the sea, and does not doubt in their heart but believes that what they say will happen, it will be done for them. Therefore, I tell you, whatever you ask for in prayer, believe that you have received it, and it will be yours."*

<u>Point of Grace</u> - Our words are powerful and cause things to manifest into the natural. Understand and believe that the words we speak matter. Speak out of your mouth by faith *"... and calleth those things which be not as thou they were," Romans 4:17*. When you are sick, speak to your body in faith, trusting God's Word and say with conviction, "I am healed." When you are struggling in your finances,

speak it into existence, "My money shall be plenty." You see, God tells us that He will meet our needs if we put Him first, and we are obedient. When we partner obedience with our belief in God's *Word*, that is what empowers what we speak to be made a reality in our lives. We can apply that principle to every aspect of our lives and every need that we have. *"If ye be willing and obedient, you shall eat the good of the land," Isaiah 1:19.*

Throughout this book, I've shared so many rich anointed scriptures from the *Word* of God. Let's plant these verses in our hearts and allow them to counsel us. Allow them to reveal the heart and mind of God while they teach our human spirit a most important lesson in how to **Believe God.**

Faith doesn't make sense to the human mind. Nor does fear make sense to the human spirit. When Jesus lived on the earth among mankind, He was one hundred percent God and one hundred percent human. He thirsted for water, felt pain, and experienced sorrow. He was despised and rejected by the very people He was willing to sacrifice His life for that all of mankind might live. *"He is despised and rejected of men; a man of sorrows, and acquainted with grief: and we hid as it were our faces from him; he was despised, and we esteemed him not," Isaiah 53:3.*

However, He chose to live by the Spirit and only believe God. Most people think Jesus was able to work miracles and had great faith because He was God. That's true. However, they don't fully understand that the human part of Jesus had to will His human flesh to be obedient to the Will and purpose that God had for Him. Jesus gave over His Will to the divine Will of God. He struggled against His flesh and disciplined His flesh to line up with the things of the Holy

Spirit. Jesus was challenged by people, grew weary, and had the same crazy emotions and weaknesses just like you and me. We know these things to be true based on the below verses found in the Bible.

"For we do not have a high priest who is unable to empathize with our weaknesses, but we have one who has been tempted in every way, just as we are—yet he did not sin," Hebrews 4:15. In fact, Jesus walked the earth as a perfect example of living a disciplined life.

As we bring this chapter to a close, I encourage you to read your Bible daily, embrace God's *Word*, and pray that God will bind your human spirit and His Holy Spirit and make them one. That is God's plan of salvation for us in that we desire to be Christ like and His Holy Spirit can make that a reality. I hope this chapter has given you some insight into the mind and heart of God and encouraged you to seek the Lord on an even more intimate level. Sincerely, I hope that training your human spirit to believe God will become your daily desire. Consider the information below as we prepare to walk into the next chapter.

Training Your Human Spirit to Believe God Past What You See

Discipline is the key to training your human spirit to believe God past what you see. With God, what we believe determines our reality. I know that as you read, meditate, and take to heart the below verses and directives, your relationship with God will be enriched, and your faith will grow to ***Believe God***.

1. **Prayer** - This is your time to talk with God. You should pray daily.

2. Proper Worship - *"Therefore, I urge you, brothers and sisters, in view of God's mercy, to offer your bodies as a living sacrifice, holy and pleasing to God—this is your true and proper worship," Romans 12:1.*
3. Meditate - *"But whose delight is in the law of the LORD, and who meditates on his law day and night," Psalm 1:2.*
4. Faith-Focused - Trust God, not what you see. What you see will deceive you. God is bigger and more powerful than all the problems, challenges, and evil that can ever come against you. *"For therein is the righteousness of God revealed from faith to faith: as it is written, the just shall live by faith," Romans 1:17.*
5. Sing – *"My lips will shout for joy when I sing praise to you – I whom you have delivered," Psalm 71:23.*
6. Godly Living - *"For the grace of God has appeared that offers salvation to all people. It teaches us to say no to ungodliness and worldly passions and to live exhibiting self-control, upright and Godly lives in this present age…" Titus 2:11-12.*
7. Study Exercise or *Word* Workout - Read and be a doer of the *Word* of God. *"But be ye doers of the word, and not hearers only, deceiving your own selves," James 1:22.*
8. Obedience – *"If ye love me, keep my commandments," John 14:15.*
9. Exercise Self-Control – *"For this very reason, make every effort to add to your faith goodness; and to goodness, knowledge; and to knowledge, self-control; and to self-control, perseverance; and to perseverance, godliness; and to godliness, mutual affection; and to mutual affection, love," 2nd Peter 1:5-8.*

10. **Spiritual Walk** - Walking by the Spirit simply means we live our lives in the continual presence of God's Spirit. The Bible tells us in *John 15:4-5*, *"Abide in me, and I in you. As the branch cannot bear fruit of itself, except it abide in the vine; no more can ye, except ye abide in me. I am the vine, ye are the branches: He that abideth in me, and I in him, the same bringeth forth much fruit: for without me ye can do nothing."* You see, when we are separated from the vine, Jesus Christ, we shrivel up and die. So let us enhance our God-consciousness and make Him the foremost in all of our affections.

11. **Thought Life** - Our thinking either sharpens or dulls our ability to believe God. *Read Proverbs 23:7, Philippians 4:8, and 2nd Corinthians 10:5.*

12. **Lose Weight** - Lay Aside Every Weight. Let's shake off any sin that dares to cling to our character and lives. We should want nothing and no one to separate us from the love of God.

13. **Work out your own salvation with fear and trembling,** *Philippians 2:12*. Let's not be confused. Working out our salvation is very different from working for our salvation. Here, Apostle Paul is simply telling us the free gift of salvation, which Christ made possible by dying on the cross for us, will show itself in your life. The inside of you will change. Those changes will come out of you and be seen in your lifestyle and your desire to be like Christ. He is telling us that the wonderful gift of salvation is inside of us. So we work out our salvation by allowing the change that happens on the inside of us to come out. In order for that to happen, we must accept Christ, His Holy Spirit, walk in faith trusting

God's *Word*, and then your Christ like character will develop and show itself.

He also is not telling us to be afraid of God. He is acknowledging that as we accept salvation and we begin to walk by faith, at first, it will be scary. But as we trust God and the transformation that He will make within our hearts and mind, our faith walk will show itself and become easier.

14. **Run the race with patience** - Be patient with yourself and don't become discouraged when you don't see quick results. We must learn to wait on God for His timing is perfect. *"But as for me, I will watch expectantly for the LORD. I will wait for the God of my salvation, My God will hear me,"* Micah 7:7.

"Then He opened their minds to understand the Scriptures."
Luke 24:45 ESV
Thank you for continuing this Spiritual literary journey with me. We are just a few chapters away from the end of our journey.

<u>Prayer</u> - I pray that God will open up the eyes to your soul that you might see Him clearly! Lord, allow us to see Your wondrous power in every situation and the circumstances that challenge us. I put my trust in You, God, for in You all things are possible.

In Jesus Name, Amen!

CHAPTER SEVEN

Take Heed Of Your Associates

Thank you so much for continuing along this insightful look into God's *Word*, His love for us, and our opportunity to know God more intimately. Let's open the door of this next chapter together and take another step closer to the connection that we want with God.

I think of salvation, which is the gift that God has for us, as the intersection where man's frailty and God's love meet. Because God loves us so much, He deeply wants to forgive us of our sins and make eternal life a reality for each of us.

In this chapter, we will discuss faith and **PFFP**. I know you're thinking what in the world is **PFFP**? I'll explain in just a minute. I wanted to poke at your curiosity first because our discussion is going to be raw and real. Let me ask you a couple of questions before we get started. Do you sometimes feel like you are not growing spiritually? Do you want to be able to hear from God and feel that you are sensitive to His voice? I think a lot people who love God and want to grow in their relationship with Him, feel that way sometimes. Maybe you are new in your walk with Christ, or you just want to know more about God. It doesn't matter why you're taking this literary journey with me. I'm just glad that you are on board.

In order to develop and grow a close relationship with God, I encourage you to consider the company that you keep. I'm talking about your friends, associates, folks that you have relationships with. Now think about my next statement with an open mind, please. When we love and care for people, we don't always recognize that they may not have the best influence on us. Sometimes people's lifestyles, the things they do or don't do, their belief system, their sense of right and wrong, and, yes, their ability to believe God can be so different from yours. When you are working toward having your life and lifestyle line up with the *Word* of God, you must give that some thought.

Just like anything else in life, sometimes we have to make some hard choices. That could mean you may need to determine if the people you call friends have a positive or negative impact on you and your ability to believe God.

It is crucial to have positive people around you when you need to **<u>Believe God</u>** for something. I call the right people **PFFP** people, and that stands for **Positive Faith-Filled People.**

Positive Faith-Filled People will stand firm and flat-footed with you in faith as they encourage you to believe God in all things. These types of strong faith-filled people will boldly tell you, "I believe God with you. It does not matter what the situation looks like. We are going to just believe." They will encourage you to continue to believe God, no matter what happens in your life.

They will share experiences of wondrous things that God has done for them. They will tell you about things that no one could have done for them but the Almighty God. And as natural as words spill out of their mouths, they will also encourage you with scriptures that they've committed to memory. They can't help it, because the *Word* of God is so powerful, and it brought them peace and comfort when nothing else could. They will help to build your faith.

(PFFP)-Positive Faith-Filled People are people of action. They are full of faith because they work their faith. As soon as they hear a negative report, they immediately begin praying faith-filled prayers over their situation and over your situation. With all confidence, they will speak life to you. Unwavering, they will proclaim that you must stand in faith and cast down the evil report in Jesus' name and only believe.

Consider the scripture in the Bible that says, *"Casting down imaginations, and every high thing that exalteth itself against the knowledge of God, and bringing into captivity every thought to the obedience of Christ," 2nd Corinthians 10:5.*

You see, by the *Word* of God, you are able to control your thoughts. The Spirit of God is powerful, and it equips and empowers us to do what we cannot do in the natural. So we can arrest unclean thoughts. We can push out of our minds sinful and evil thoughts that dare to tempt us to think, say, or do wrong things. And when you surround yourself with the right company, those who are positive and filled with faith, you are equally yoked, since they are striving for the same control by the Spirit of God.

(PFFP)-Positive Faith-Filled People are not wishy-washy. You know what I mean, the kind of folks who believe with you one minute, but when the situation turns for the worst, they abandon you. Those are the folks who say to others behind your back, "She needs to face reality. The doctor said her condition is terminal, and she's dying. Maybe it's just her time to go or it's the Will of God." NO! God wants His people to be healthy and flourish in life. God's *Word* assures me of that in ***3rd John 1:2, "Beloved, I wish above all things that you may prosper and be in health, even as your soul prospers."***

Positive Faith-Filled People are companions who hold fast with you to their confession of faith and trust in God because they know and believe the scriptures. The scripture tells us in ***Hebrews 10:23, "Let us hold fast the confession of our hope without wavering, for He who promised is faithful."*** This verse is telling us that we can trust God. What He promises us, He is sure to honor and bring those things to pass in our lives.

When we are oppressed and depressed by challenging, sorrowful, and life-altering situations, we need those faithful few who will stand with us and trust God to answer prayers. Those who will believe God with you for what they cannot see. Their prayers are aggressive, bold, and powerful as they stand steadfast and unmovable in their faith in God. They stand firm as they battle with you against all the powers of hell and darkness. The scriptures tell us, *"As iron sharpens iron, so one person sharpens another," Proverbs 27:17.* Hold onto your faith and surround yourself with people of faith.

Examine a couple of accounts in the Bible below that reveal the magnificent and powerful God that we love. Throughout our journey in this book, we have talked about growing our faith in God, learning how to stand on the *Word* of God, and believe Him past what you see. We know now that faith is a process and that as we exercise our faith in God, our faith muscle gets stronger and stronger. Read the accounts below for yourself. Don't just take my word for it. Read and search the scriptures for yourself, and you will see the significant role that faith played in each miracle below. You will also see how God will bless when we have little faith in an effort that our faith might grow.

1. Jesus healed a blind man in a very unexpected way. He spat on the man's eyes as a way of healing him. The scripture reads, *"And he took the blind man by the hand, and led him out of town; and when he had spit on his eyes, and put his hands upon him, he asked him if he saw ought. And he looked up and said, 'I see men as trees walking.' After that He put his hands again upon his eyes, and made him look up: and he was restored, and saw every man clearly," Mark 8:23-25.* In the natural, you would probably be repulsed by someone spitting on any part of your body. We don't have to understand what God tells us to do. We just need to have faith and be obedient; it is then that we will see the incomparable power of God.

2. Jesus commanded the storm to be still. Read the account. *"And when he was entered into a ship, his disciples followed him. And, behold, there arose a great tempest in the sea, insomuch that the ship was covered with the waves: but he was asleep. And his disciples came to him, and awoke him, saying, Lord, save us: we perish. And he saith unto them, Why are ye fearful, O ye of little faith? Then he arose, and rebuked the winds and the sea; and there was a great calm. But the men marveled,*

saying, What manner of man is this, that even the winds and the sea obey him!" Matthew 8:23-27.

What manner of man is this? He is the Almighty God. Even the elements must obey the voice of God. If He can command the wind and the sea, surely he can command the challenges in your life to be still. I know I don't want to be the one that God labels as "Ye of little faith."

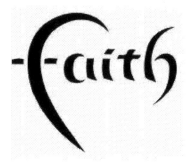

See how faith in God can bring about a transformation in the most desperate circumstances. Those who walk in faith, we expect the unbelievable to transpire because of the believable God that we serve. It doesn't matter if the doctor diagnosed you with an incurable disease and told you that you only have a few months to live. It doesn't matter that you lost your job. Maybe you feel like your marriage is on the brink of divorce. Maybe you feel depressed; you can't explain why. Sometimes people are so overwhelmed by the challenges and tragedies in life; they start to feel that life isn't worth living. They consider suicide.

Those are very real and devastating life challenges that someone is going through right now, even as you read this book. I am here to tell you and that person, whoever they are, and where ever they are, God has the ultimate say. God is the creator of all life. He knows every beat of your heart, every ounce of blood that courses through your veins, and every strand of hair on your head, He knows specifically. God is a healer! He can heal your body, your finances, and your marriage. He can heal any and everything. He simply wants you to come to Him and have faith in His *Word* and His power. Embrace this verse and remember it when the winds of adversity are blowing in your life.

"Blessed is the man that maketh the LORD his trust...," Psalm 40:4.

<u>Point of Grace</u> - Because we want and need to grow in our faith, it is important for us to surround ourselves with **PFFP**. Let's revisit Jairus' experience for a minute. We discussed him back in chapter 3. I noticed something about Jairus. He had the wrong type of people around him. Yes, I said it. He had the wrong type of people around him as he desperately needed Jesus to bless his daughter. Why? The people around him were doubters, death speaking people; they were a hindrance to his ability to **believe** Jesus for a miracle. In chapter 3, we talked about the miracle Jesus performed when He raised Jairus' daughter from the dead. Keep in mind that before Jesus did that, He put the unbelievers in the room out. They did not have an opportunity to witness Jesus' miraculous power over death.

Only the child's parents and three of Jesus' disciples, Peter, James, and John, were able to witness the power of Jesus. Jairus had a measure of faith in Jesus because he had gone to Jesus and asked Him to help his daughter. Of course, he had no idea how his faith was going to be tested when Jesus said, *"The child is not dead but sleeping," Matthew 9:24.* The disciples with Jesus knew His wondrous powers and weren't standing there doubting His ability beyond any natural man. This is a clear example that we need to be selective of the company that we keep, especially when we need to have faith in God to address our problems, or do what we think is a hard thing.

Proverbs 13:20 tells us, "Whoever walks with the wise becomes wise, but the companion of fools will suffer harm." Remember the question that Jairus was asked before him and Jesus arrived at his home? *"Thy daughter is dead: why troublest thou the Master any further?" Mark 5:35.*

Those were not words of faith. And they were surely not words that would have been spoken by **Positive Faith-Filled People**. Not at all! Jairus was told don't trouble Jesus. Basically, don't concern Jesus with your problem. Jesus can't help you. Her situation is hopeless, and it's time to start planning your daughter's funeral.

The desperate father needed someone around him to encourage his faith. Someone who would have said, "This is the time to trust Jesus. He is a way maker, a healer with power to do the impossible." He fed over five thousand people with five loaves of bread and two fishes, and there was still food left over. Read the account in *Matthew 14:13-21.*

Jairus needed to hear someone say to him, "This is the time to tell the one who was with God in the beginning; the one who can make a difference, tell Him what you need. The *Word* proclaims, *"And the Lord God formed man of the dust of the ground, and breathed into his nostrils the breath of life; and man became a living soul," Genesis 2:7.* Only Jesus is capable of doing all of that. He can also raise your daughter up."

Mark 5: 39-40 tells us that **Ado** People were in Jairus' house. Not **(PFFP)-Positive Faith-Filled People**. Don't buddy up with **Ado** people. Put them out and Only Believe God. Not sure what the word **Ado** means? Simple, the Greek meaning is – <u>making noise</u>. The folks in Jairus' house were making the wrong noise; they made commotional sounds of hopelessness, sounds that troubled the mind and heart, and caused confusion. Hear me when I say, be selective about the company that you keep.

The people in Jairus' home were there to comfort him. They were probably family and friends. With family and friends, we really have to be watchful of their words. We know most of them mean well, but be careful and listen to what they say to you in times when you need to believe God and in general. The wrong noise will confuse you into thinking what they are saying is in your best interest. However, in reality, it is a stumbling block for you. They are being influenced by the devil and about to make you miss your blessing.

Bad company can harm our judgment, belief in God, and our ability to trust Him. *"Do not be misled: Bad company corrupts good character," 1st Corinthians 15:33*. It is not difficult to believe that having friends around you with bad characters can influence you in many ways. That is why parents are concerned about their children knowing how to choose positive friends. *"Whoever walks with the wise becomes wise, but the companion of fools will suffer harm."* I didn't say it, the *Word* of God did. Please, read it for yourself in *Proverbs 13:20*. We need to be concerned and cautious about the company that we keep.

If bad company corrupts good behavior, then being in the company of those that don't believe God can corrupt your beliefs. If we sit in the company of fools, eventually, we will begin acting like fools. If you keep company with those who have to see it before they can believe God, they will affect your ability to believe God beyond what you can see. Jesus told Thomas, who did not believe, Jesus had risen from the grave, *"Thomas, because thou hast seen me, thou hast believed: blessed are they that have not seen, and yet have believed," John 20:29.* Bad Company corrupts good behavior. It can cause you to stumble and walk in the darkness of incorrect thinking and sin.

Good parents will always checkout their children's friends; they will want to know who they spend their time with. In addition, they will want to know something about the kid's parents. Those are the type of parents who will guide their children and counsel them on the qualities that make a good friend. If our children's friends are running with gangs, a good parent will instruct their child not to associate with that person, because they are a bad influence. I encourage you to leave the <u>doubters</u> and cleave to <u>believers,</u> or you will be influenced by their unbelief. I think this is a great instructional verse laced with wisdom. *"Leave the presence of a fool, for there you do not meet words of knowledge," Proverbs, 14:7.*

We can't walk shoulder to shoulder and buddy up with everyone if we want to grow our faith in God. People's words will get into our spirit, start messing with our mind, what we believe, hinder our ability to trust God for a hard thing, and cause us to miss our blessings. That's why when Jesus heard the dreadful proclamation made to Jairus that his daughter was dead, He immediately directed Jairus according to what his thoughts should be. Jesus said, *"Be not afraid, only believe," Mark 5:36.* Our thoughts and our words are powerful. But nothing and no one is more powerful than God Almighty. Just like you get up and put clothes on every day, you need to cloth your heart and your mind every day. Cloth and saturate

them with the right thoughts and the anointed *Word* of God. Enhance that clothing by surrounding yourself with people who would be considered good company, **(PFFP)-Positive Faith Filled People**. When you do these things, you will find yourself in the right environment to grow your faith in God, and you can knit that cloak of faith that you desire. As we leave this chapter and prepare to step into the next, I leave you with the below thought.

<u>Say it with me "In the Process - Put Them Out - and Only Believe."</u>

"O God, thou art my God; early will I see thee: my soul thirsteth for thee, my flesh longeth for thee in a dry and thirsty land, where no water is; to see thy power and thy glory…"
Psalm 63:1-3

Seek God in all that you do. Give Him praise in all things, great and small.

<u>Prayer</u> - Precious God, whom I love, I thank You for the goodness and mercy that You show me each and every day. Thank You for helping me to make the right decisions in life. Lord, I need You to help me to be wise and choose **Positive Faith-Filled People** to surround myself with.
You are truly an awesome God!
In Jesus Name, Amen!

CHAPTER EIGHT
Believe God For Bigger Better

"Now to him who is able to do immeasurably more than all we ask or imagine, according to his power that is at work within us," Ephesians 3:20.

In 2015, I heard in my spirit two words, **Bigger Better**. I assumed these two words were mostly for a bigger better church facility because at the time that was on my heart. However, God wasn't only referring to our church. God wanted me to grow in my faith and in my thinking over and above what I could have ever imagined. He meant that I needed a bigger better ability to believe Him for everything I needed, wanted, and the very blessings He had already destined for me. That bigger better growth included faith, healing, provision, miracles, revelation knowledge of Him, and more.

On January 1st, 2016, God began to open up my understanding and gave me insight and revelation to share with the body of Christ. He made it clear to me how just two words, **Bigger Better**, when used in faith, they will cause the kingdom of God to manifest in our life right here on earth. The words **Bigger Better** will bring us into the fullness of God's blessings. If we are able to believe God, we will receive over and above all that we ask or think according to the power that is at work within us.

Now don't miss the last part of our foundational scripture, *Ephesians 3:20*, because once you receive the revelation of the last part of this scripture, you will believe God for the **Bigger Better**. *"...According to His power that is at work within you."*

You see, God has given us an internal helper and working power so that He can do **Bigger Better** things through the body of believers. The power of the Holy Ghost is the power that Apostle Paul was talking about in *Ephesians 3:20*. I like the Good News translation of the verse. *"To him who by means of the power working in us is able to do so much more than we can ever ask for, or even think of."* The power of the Holy Spirit is working in us to bring about so much more than what we ask or think. Jesus promised in *John 14:15-27* that the Holy Spirit will be our helper, and will live within us. He promised that we would know the Holy Spirit, and the Holy Spirit will be at work in our lives, teaching us all things, reminding us what Jesus has said, and that same Spirit will never leave us. Right now, the power of the Holy Spirit resides within us and is enabling us to grow in our faith. God's Holy

Spirit will lead us to all truths about God. So we will believe God to do the immeasurable more than all we
ask or can imagine.

God wants us to imagine **Bigger Better**, because He's a big God. He is Jehovah-Jireh, our provider, and has bigger better plans for our life. It will take bigger better faith and bigger better thinking to receive all He has planned for us. And not only that, God requires us to become acquainted with the Holy Spirit. Why is that a necessity? It is an absolute necessity for us to be connected with God and be on one accord with Him. The power within us will change the world around us.

When our believing lines up with God's *Word*, the power of God within us is explosive! God is pleased when we have big faith because faith is the beginning of something bigger and better in our life. *Proverbs 23:7, "For as he thinketh in his heart, so is he."*

What is the Bigger Better that you need God to work in your life? Increased anointing, spiritual gifts, a better job, a spouse, money, homeownership, salvation for your children, spouse or loved ones, good health, it could be any of those things or something else. It doesn't matter what it is since God can give that to you and more. Believe Him for it. The *Word* of God is so rich with instructions for us, which helps us to know the heart and mind of God and builds our faith. *"The thief comes not but that he may steal, and kill, and destroy: I am come that they might have life, and might have [it] abundantly," John 10:10.* What is the heart of this verse? It means in Christ, you can live your life more fully. You have in Christ, and by His Grace, the ability to love, to be at peace, to enrich the lives of others, to overcome evil, and to be free to a greater degree than without Jesus. It is the power of God that can change the world for the better. It also means that those in Christ will experience greatness in life more than we can even imagine.

Have you figured out what opens the door to the **Bigger Better?** There has been a thread of continuity throughout this book. Each chapter has led us to Christ. The thread of knowledge uncovered in each chapter has woven one blanket of truth; we need God's Holy Spirit. It is the Holy Spirit that binds us to God.

The trail of biblical insight that we've uncovered throughout each chapter are elements that equip us to grow in God. They are steps that help us walk into the **Bigger Better.** We've talked about all of the below:

1. Do You Believe God
2. God Is A Spirit
3. Only Believe
4. I Believe God Even When He Is Quiet
5. I Believe God And The Power Of Prayer
6. Training Your Human Spirit To Believe God
7. Take Heed Of Your Associates

When we are accepting of those things, understand them, and partner them with the power of the Holy Spirit, we have the key to walk through the door of **Bigger Better.**

Let's consider the power within the **Holy Spirit.** The Holy Spirit is the third person of the Trinity, which is the Father, Son, and Holy Spirit. He lives in the temple (the body) of all followers of Christ. Jesus promised He would ask the Father to give us a Helper, the (Holy Spirit), which will empower followers of Christ and abide within them forever.

"I will ask the Father, and He will give you another Helper that He may be with you forever; the Spirit of truth, whom the world cannot receive, because it does not behold Him or know Him, but you know Him because He abides with you, and will be in you. I will not leave you as orphans; I will come to you," John 14:16-18.

We need to understand; the Holy Spirit serves a specific purpose in our lives. Consider the below ways God's Spirit can impact your Christian walk.

Roles of the Holy Spirit:

- To divinely empower us to be true disciples of Christ.
- Equip us to be effective witnesses of Jesus Christ.
- Be a Comforter to us.
- Encourage and counsel us.
- Be a teacher of all truth.
- Strengthen us and empower us to obey God's Will and live holy.
- Remind us of God's *Word* as it impacts our mind, heart and lifestyle.
- Reveal the future to us.
- Cultivate within our lives the fruits of the Spirit: (love, joy, peace, forbearance, kindness, goodness, faithfulness, gentleness and self-control), ***Galatians 5:22-23.***

If the Holy Spirit is who empowers us and is our abiding helper and teacher, then it's important that we understand the purpose of the Holy Spirit and acknowledge His presence in our lives daily. It is critical that we build a personal and growing relationship with the Holy

Spirit. Keep in mind that it is the Holy Spirit that binds us to God and makes the Bigger Better possible.

Bigger Better in God is a choice. Have you already chosen a path for your life? Maybe you are pursuing that path with a passion. At some point in your life, you will have to choose God or the ordinary old life that the world has to offer. When you choose God, you are destined for Bigger Better. When God unveils His vision for your life, things change; you change, your priorities change, you then truly have a purposeful life.

I love the example of Apostle Paul and his **Bigger Better** life. If you know anything about the Bible's New Testament, then surely you know about the dynamic and anointed Apostle Paul. He was a self-appointed persecutor of the church. At that time, his name was Saul. He wholeheartedly believed those who were teaching that Jesus Christ was the Messiah were teaching heresy, which is teaching something that is false. In Saul's mind, Jesus couldn't be the Messiah, since He was crucified, hung on a cross, and died. He believed those teaching that He was bound in the earth by death for three days and then rose from the dead to have all power, and calling himself the risen Christ; the savior of all man-kind were spreading lies and false doctrine. It was absolutely absurd to Saul. That drove his plan to pursue and drag off to prison those that taught such heresy.

But God changed the course of his life with a different plan. Saul was on the road to Damascus determined to find the false teachers in that city, and off to prison he would take them. It was on this road that Saul had a conversion experience. *"And as he journeyed, he came near Damascus: and suddenly there shined round about him a light from heaven: And he fell to the earth, and heard a voice saying unto him,*

Saul, Saul, why persecutest thou me? And he said, Who art thou, Lord? And the Lord said, I am Jesus whom thou persecutest: it is hard for thee to kick against the pricks," Acts 9:1-5.

Wow, what a life-changing experience Saul walked into on his journey to destroy God's people. Because of this experience, his name was changed to Paul. He became one of the most dynamic and impactful followers of Christ and wrote two-thirds of the Bible's New Testament. Paul then walked into the **Bigger Better** life that God had for him. Read the full account of his miraculous conversion in *Acts 9:1-31*.

You see, we will all come to a fork in the road on our life's journey. It is then that we will either choose to accept the plan God has for us or follow the leading of our flesh and attempt to navigate life using our own plan. I don't know about you, but as for me and my house, we will serve the Lord. I choose **Bigger Better** and desire the good hand of God to orchestrate my life.

Expect God's Promises

Along with God's Bigger Better purpose for our lives, we should expect God to fulfill all His hundreds of promises for our specific needs. Those many promises include spiritual blessings, and a few others include abundant grace, forgiveness, righteousness, free access to God through Christ, hope, happiness, peace, joy in the Holy Ghost, eternal life, and bountiful spiritual blessings.

God's promises also include living an abundant good life full of abounding joy in the flesh here on earth. These promises are God's plan, and everyone that accepts Jesus as Lord and Savior should expect to enjoy all the promises of God. *"Every good and perfect gift is from above, coming down from the Father of the heavenly lights, who does not change like shifting shadows," James 1:17.*

The thief, which is the devil, comes in many forms to seize and take away through deception, deceit, and false doctrine what rightfully belongs to the believer in Christ. Through the back door of deception, the devil steals the believer's prayer life, study time, passion for God, health, joy, finances, etc. The life that Jesus promises is spiritual, natural, and eternal. Don't allow the devil to steal the promises and blessings God has for you.

Let's examine some scriptures about the covenant agreement God made with Abram that tells us the reason why we should expect the bigger better. God called Abram out of his country and his father's house to go into a strange land that he knew nothing about. Abram left his country at age seventy-five with all of his possessions. He also took his nephew, Lot, with him into this strange land.

Genesis 12:1-3, *"GOD told Abram, Leave your country, your family, and your father's home for a land that I will show you. I'll make you a great nation and bless you. I'll make you famous; you'll be a blessing. I'll bless those who bless you; those who curse you, I'll curse. All the families of the Earth will be blessed through you."*

You and I must also allow only God to lead us, just as Abram did. When we follow the leading of the Lord, bountiful blessings will come to us. God's rich *Word* promises us, *"If you are willing and obedient, you shall eat the good of the land," Isaiah 1:19.* Your present situation may look the same or get worse while you obey and believe God for the **Bigger Better**. It did for Abram. As he obeyed God and walked by faith, he also knew the land God promised his descendants was filled with Canaanites; a strong nation of people. The Bible says, *"Abram* *passed through the country as far as Shechem and the Oak of Moreh. At that time the Canaanites occupied the land," Genesis 12:6.* Yet Abram continued to believe God's promises that they would possess the land. Along the journey to Canaan, Abram stopped to pray and worship God, *Genesis 12:7, 8.*

On our journey to believing God for the bigger better, we also need to pray and worship God amid our desert place. Your **Bigger Better** is just over the horizon.

It's important that you stop, worship, and sacrifice your time and focus before God in prayer. Tell Him how much you love Him; stop and rejoice in the Lord; stop and praise Him in song. Worshiping helps us take our mind off our problems and put our focus on God. Our joy in Him will become our strength. As we walk in obedience, there will be confusing, hard, and dry seasons in life. But if we worship during these seasons, we will experience God's peace, wisdom, and direction, as we believe God for the bigger better.

We all want to live a fruitful and blessed life here on earth. We also want the eternal life with God that is promised to us if we live for him here on earth. It is vital for you to know that the **Bigger Better** life is not just to benefit you alone. God wants to use you to witness to others and be a blessing to others. I think the below two scriptures truly makes that point clear. *"Go ye therefore, and teach all nations, baptizing them in the name of the Father, and of the Son, and of the Holy Ghost. Teaching them to observe all things whatsoever I have commanded you: and, lo, I am with you always, even unto the end of the world. Amen," Matthew 28: 19-20.* And the following verse speaks to the impact your life can have on others. *"Ye are our epistle written in our hearts, known and read of all men," 2nd Corinthians 3:2.*

An epistle is a letter. When we give our lives to Christ, our life is like an open letter for all to see. The world can read our lives and see clearly if our actions and lifestyle is Christ like since that is what the word Christian means. Now let's be honest and straight forward. Some letters are pleasant to witness, and there are some that make you question their credibility. Meaning some folks who call themselves Christians don't live lifestyles that line up with God's *Word*. The letter of their lives is not pleasant for others to read. And their lives are not drawing others to Christ. That is not the example that I want to be.

The life that you live could very well be the drawing card that someone needs to trust that God can change their life, the way He changed yours. God wants to use our **Bigger Better** life to show someone the path to Christ and that their own **Bigger Better** life is waiting for them in Christ.

Often you hear people say, "I don't know what my calling is. I'm just not sure what God would have me to do." All Christians need to understand that we all share one common calling on our lives given to us by God. *"The Lord said to the servant, Go out into the highways and hedges, and compel them to come in, that my house may be filled," Luke 14:23.* There it is; you can stop wondering now. Until God adds to your commission with other callings upon your life, that is the work which He has called you to do. **<u>Go out and compel them to come.</u>**

Your new life in Christ, your new way of thinking, your changed lifestyle, your understanding and hunger for God's *Word*, and your new heart and mind, which enables you to forgive and love the un-loveable, will have sculpted you into the Bigger Better you. Imagine a Bigger Better ability to love like Christ loves and to forgive like Christ. All of us have a measure of love to give. But how deep does your ability to forgive run?

Can you forgive those that hurt you with intentional malice? Infidelity, mental and physical abuse, someone beating or molesting a child, murder; how do you forgive those types of betrayals and horrible acts? Only God can give you that type of bigger better heart. Allowing Christ to change you makes you that vessel that He can use.

<u>Point of Grace</u> – *"The thief does not come except to steal, and to kill, and to destroy. I have come that they might have life, and that they may have it more abundantly," John 10:10.* In my mind, we are to present Christ as life to the world. In Christ is how we truly have an abundant life.

As born again believers and sons and daughters of God, we have covenant rights, privileges, and full entitlement to claim everything that God has promised us in His *Word*. Yes, that includes the **Bigger Better**. Understanding our covenant rights (God's agreement with man and the promises that are ours to claim) is vitally important. Some believers don't understand their covenant rights, and because they don't understand, they have no strong foundation to stand on for receiving the benefits that God promises to us.

A Covenant is a contract or agreement between all involved parties that requires some action on behalf of each person. God will never violate His agreement with us. His *Word* assures us of it. *"I will not violate my covenant or alter what my lips have uttered," Psalm, 89:34.* As sons of God, we are guaranteed according to this scripture that God will keep His promise to us. God cannot tell a lie, ***Numbers 23:19***. If He said it, He will perform His *Word*.

"If ye abide in me, and my words abide in you, ye shall ask what ye will, and it shall be done unto you," John 15:7. This verse has two criteria - Abide in Christ (stay in His love) and in His *Word* (obey His

Word). As we abide in his *Word* our faith grows to receive answered prayers. Keep in mind, faith cometh by hearing the *Word* of God over and over again. Abiding in Christ means to line our lives up with God's *Word* while living daily according to His *Word*. We abide in Christ by keeping His commandments. *"If you keep my commandments, you will abide in my love, just as I have kept my Father's commandments and abide in his love," John 15:10.* Please consider that verse and also *John 15:5, "I am the vine, ye are the branches: He that abideth in me, and I in him, the same bringeth forth much fruit: for without me ye can do nothing."* Now you have the whole picture, both pieces of the puzzle. God is our substance, and in Him we have our being.

As we abide in Christ, the fruitful blessings and anointed gifts of God are sure to come to us. There are some blessings that we have to wait for the Lord to give us. But there is also Bigger Better blessings that God wants to bless us with right NOW! Not in one of these days or in the bye and bye. We must be good stewards over our words.

Many people are not receiving their blessings now because of what they are saying now. Our words are powerful; they can be a blessing to us now, and life-giving now. Our words can even bring into existence what we want to see manifested in our life now or delay our blessings. I have spoken words that were actually manifested only for me to end up regretting having spoken them. Sometimes we carelessly use words without realizing the damage those words can cause. For example, sometimes out of frustration, people will say, "I'm sick to death of this or that." Those are very strong words, and you are actually speaking death over yourself.

Please read and consider the below verses that speak volumes about how careful we should be in our choice of words.

1. *"A person's words can be a source of wisdom, deep as the ocean, fresh as a flowing stream," Proverbs 18:4.*
2. *"Whoever guards his mouth preserves his life; he who opens wide his lips comes to ruin," Proverbs 13:3.*
3. *"Death and life are in the power of the tongue, and those who love it will eat its fruits," Proverbs 18:21.*

The wise counsel of the above verses makes them valuable pearls for us to hold onto. For example, we should always say if it be thou Will. Why? It is because those who put their trust in the Lord want to be led by the Lord. They want their will to line up with His Will. That is imperative in order to walk in the Bigger Better. When Jesus was preparing to go to the cross and die for the sins of all humanity, He prayed to the Father, saying *"...Father, if thou be willing, remove this cup from me: nevertheless, not my will, but thine, be done," Luke 22:42.*

Our human nature wants what it wants when it wants it. That makes it difficult sometimes for us to seek the Will of God and push aside our own plans for what we desire or want to do. But if Jesus can give His Will over to God, when His flesh did not want to die on the cross, surely, we can let God lead us when our plans and desires don't compare to the sacrifice of Christ going to the cross.

I remember once praying about an event that I was planning and thought I was praying a prayer of faith. I was excited and praying with authority as I told God what I wanted to be done, and how I wanted Him to do it. I prayed in great detail. Jesus knew I meant well and lovingly spoke to me, saying "What about my plans for the event? I have plans too." Wow! The words Jesus spoke to me had an immediate impact on my heart and mindset. I realized I was praying selfishly for my gratification. I had given no thought to what God desired for the event. I was absorbed in my thoughts and plans. But I want everything that I do to be done unto the purpose and Will of God that He might be exalted. Immediately, I changed my prayer to God, and I added, "If it be your Will."

Consider this verse, *"Therefore do not be foolish, but understand what the will of the Lord is," Ephesians 5:17.*

We must know what the Will of God is for our lives. So that our plans and desires are not foolish, but according to God's Will.

There is value in what you say, and we have to claim the Bigger Better by our words and actions. Why? Because our thoughts become our words, and our words become our actions. So as we walk into the Bigger Better, let's choose our words carefully and speak into existence that which is not as though it is.

I encourage you to look to God for your Bigger Better in the natural and in the spiritual. Great things await you along life's path. Those great things, all of them, are allowed and orchestrated by Christ and fueled by your faith.

Thank you for completing this Biblical and Spiritual journey with me. As we come to the end of this particular path, know that your journey is not over. Our desire to grow in God, understand His heart and mind, and genuinely appreciate His *Word* is a daily pursuit. And it is not just for us alone. The knowledge and understanding that we gain is a treasure that God requires us to share with others.

Your journey doesn't stop here at the end of this book. The Bible tells us, *"Study to show thyself approved unto God, a workman that needeth not to be ashamed, rightly dividing the word of truth,"*

2nd Timothy 2:15. Now that you have taken this literary journey with me and opened the door to your mind and heart to know God better and walk in the Bigger Better because of that knowledge, you are ready to continue to uncover all the treasures that God has for you in His rich *Word*.

As you live your life and walk through the many valleys of decisions that you will face, I hope you will choose Christ. It is in the more abundant life that God has promised us that the Bigger Better resides.

"For in him we live, and move, and have our being..."
Acts 17:28

<u>Prayer</u> - Mighty, powerful, and all-knowing God, thank You for the love that You have for me, and the awesome plan You have for my life. I desire that You lead and guide me down the path that You have carved out just for me. I will follow You blindly because I trust that You know what is best for me. Help me to be obedient to Your *Word* and direction even when I don't understand. I know that if I follow You into the unknown, You will make things clear to me in due time.
In You, I have my being; I live and move,
by Your Grace. I truly know there are
Bountiful Blessings in Believing!
In Jesus Name, Amen!

Made in the USA
Monee, IL
22 September 2020